CROATIA

Robert Cooper

MARSHALL CAVENDISH
New York • London • Sydney

Reference edition published 2001 by
Marshall Cavendish Corporation
99 White Plains Road
Tarrytown
New York 10591

© Times Media Private Limited 2000

Originated and designed by
Times Books International, an imprint of
Times Media Private Limited, a member of the
Times Publishing Group

Printed in Malaysia

Library of Congress Cataloging-in-Publication Data:

Cooper, Robert.
   Croatia / Robert Cooper.
      p. cm. — (Cultures of the world)
   Cover title.
   Includes bibliographical references and index.
   ISBN 0-7614-1156-9
   1. Croatia—Juvenile literature.   [1. Croatia.]   I. Title. II.
Series.
   DR1510 .C66 2001
   949.72—dc21

                00-029510
                CIP
                AC

INTRODUCTION

THE REPUBLIC OF CROATIA and its people have survived against the odds. The country has been invaded and divided and its people suppressed and divided with such regularity that full independence was finally achieved only on October 8, 1991.

Croatians see themselves forever poised on a civilization divide. This precarious position has perhaps prompted them to make their presence known to the world. Indeed, Croatia has certainly had an influence on Europe and the Americas far in excess of its size and the size of its population.

The people of this remarkable little country has excelled in the arts and sciences. Its famous sons include inventor Nikola Tesla and sculptor Ivan Meštrović. Within an area of 21, 824 square miles (56,538 square km), visitors will find fertile plains, snow-capped mountains, and spectacular waterfalls.

CONTENTS

Italian influences can be seen in the art and architecture of Rovinj, a town on the west coast of Istria.

CONTENTS

A **Croatian's** traditional dress reflects her region. The most colorful and richly embroidered costumes are found in the Pannonian region.

GEOGRAPHY

CROATIA, a crescent-shaped country situated in the northwest of the Balkan peninsula, has a total land area of 21,824 square miles (56,538 square km), slightly smaller than West Virginia. About 2,849 square miles (4,584 square km) of the land are protected nature reserves.

The country shares 1,260 miles (2,027 km) of land border with five countries: Slovenia and Hungary in the north, Bosnia and Herzegovina and Serbia in the east, and Montenegro in the south. It also shares sea borders with Slovenia, Montenegro, and Italy.

The republic is made up of three historical regions—Croatia-Slavonia in the north, Istria on the Istrian peninsula, and Dalmatia, which lies along the Adriatic coast.

The vicious wars that marked the breakup of the former Yugoslavia did little damage to the splendors of Croatia's natural environment and spared most of its historic cities, apart from Dubrovnik and Vukovar.

Left: **The island of Mljet, west of Dubrovnik. Ancient Greeks referred to it as** *Melita***, or "honey," because its forests were full of wild bees.**

Opposite: **A coastal view of the walled city of Dubrovnik in southern Dalmatia. This jewel in Croatia's crown attracts many tourists to the Dalmatian coast.**

"The gods wanted to crown their creation, and on the last day they turned tears, stars, and the sea breeze into the isles of Kornati."

George Bernard Shaw on Croatia, the largest archipelago in the Mediterranean Sea.

TOPOGRAPHY

Geographically, Croatia is divided into three parts—the Adriatic coast in the southwest where mountains slope into the Adriatic Sea and emerge as more than 1,000 islands; the Dinaric Alps, mountain range stretching from northwest to southeast; and the Pannonian Plain in the north and north-eastern part of the country.

THE ADRIATIC COAST

The Adriatic coast, which extends from the Gulf of Venice to the Gulf of Kotor, is one of the most irregular coastlines in the world, a fact that has given us the term "Dalmatian-type coast." Croatia's 1,105 miles (1,778 km) of Adriatic coastline is bordered by 1,185 islands—the largest archipelago in the Mediterranean Sea.

Only 66 islands are inhabited year-round. The largest are Cres, Krk, Pag, Rab, and Lošinj along the northern coast; Dugi Otok, Kornat, Ugljan, and Pašman in the center; and Brač, Hvar, Korčula, Pelješac, and Mljet in the south. About 100 islands are temporarily occupied during the tourist or fishing seasons; the remaining 1,000 are uninhabited.

The indented coastline of Split, the second largest city in Croatia.

Winter in the Plitvice Lakes, perhaps the most beautiful of Croatia's many national parks. The area is known for its stunning lakes and breathtaking waterfalls.

THE DINARIC ALPS

Rising steeply from the turquoise sea and yellow beaches, the Dinaric Alps follow the coastal northwest-southeast finger of Croatia and continue into neighboring Bosnia and Herzegovina, where some of the highest peaks are found. In Croatia the mountains are usually several hundred feet below the highest peak, Mount Dinara, which stands 6,006 feet (1,830 meters) above sea level. This region has a unique geological feature—a terrace made of karst, a soft limestone that is easily eroded into unusual shapes. Also found in the mountains are the *Plitvička Jezera*, or Plitvice Lakes. These 16 lakes, connected by 92 waterfalls, are thought to have been formed 4,000 years ago. They were placed on United Nations Educational, Scientific, and Cultural Organization's (UNESCO) list of world natural heritage sites in 1979.

THE PANNONIAN PLAIN

Mountains rise steeply from the coast, then slope away in the north of Croatia to the Pannonian Plain. It was so named because in prehistory, the area formed the inland Pannonian Sea. Today the shallow Lake Balaton in Hungary is the last remnant of this ancient sea.

The flat plains, which are located between the Sava and Drava rivers, are the most fertile part of the country due to the alluvial soil from the two rivers. The area is referred to as the "Croatian granary," and produces high yields of wheat, corn, sugar beet, sunflowers, alfalfa, and clover. There is a saying that the farmers and culture of the region are as rich as the soil. The region also has oil and gas deposits.

Peasants with an oxcart loaded with corn.

Above: **Bears are frequently spotted in the Croatian countryside.**

Right: **While 23% of Croatia is covered by forests, it is estimated that 50% of the trees are threatened by acid rain generated by Croatia's industrialized neighbors.**

FLORA AND FAUNA

Plants and animals that have disappeared in other parts of Europe have survived in Croatia. This is partly due to the fact that natural resources have not been overdeveloped because of the comparatively low population density. Another reason is that many areas have been designated national parks or special reserves, where hunting and collecting are forbidden. Thus, Croatia is the refuge of the endangered griffon vulture; perhaps its last colony is on the island of Cres.

Other, more abundant, fauna includes bears, wolves, long-eared owls, chamois, lynx, deer, and marsh birds. Endemic insects and reptiles have survived the onslaught of European industrialization and national wars and have multiplied in Croatia.

The mountains, hillsides, and gorges provide a large quantity of wood from beech, oak, ash, cherry, and black pine trees. This is used by the

domestic furniture industry and exported in the form of furniture and parquet flooring to the rest of Europe and the United States. The most abundant plant life is in the Velebit mountain range, where 2,700 species, among them the edelweiss, and more than 70 plants native to the region have been counted.

In contrast, a different type of vegetation can be found along the Adriatic coast, where cypresses, laurels, oleanders, aloes, and olive and fig trees thrive. Some 4,300 plant species have been identified on the coast and farther inland. More than 360 species of fish can be found in Croatia's clear waters. There are also sponges and corals.

THE GRIFFON VULTURE

Only 150 griffon vultures remain in Croatia; most live on the cliffs of Cres island. A full-grown griffon measures about 3 feet (1 m) from wingtip to wingtip, weighs approximately 18 pounds (8 kg), and can reach flying speeds of up to 75 miles per hour (120 km per hour).

Griffon vultures live in colonies and fly in a widespread formation looking for animal carcasses, mainly dead sheep. When food is spied by one bird, it circles, signaling the rest of the formation.

The griffon does not enjoy official protection as an endangered species in Croatia. However, Croatian farmers look kindly on them as they dispose of dead sheep, thus preventing disease or infection from spreading to other livestock. To harm a griffon is considered very bad luck.

The Velebit Mountains are part of the Dinaric Alps. The highest point is the Vaganski peak at 5,766 feet (1,757m).

CLIMATE

The three geographic belts of Croatia have distinct climates. The Adriatic coast enjoys long, warm summers, when high temperatures are cooled by sea breezes to an average 77°F (25°C), and short, mild winters, when the heat stored in the sea during the summer warms the land. January temperatures range from 41°F (5°C) to 50°F (10°C). The Pannonian region has a continental climate of cold winters and hot summers. The Dinaric Alps endure an Alpine climate of long, cold winters and short summers; even on the coldest day when snow covers the land, the sun often shines.

There are four significant winds in Croatia. The strongest is the *bura*, a northeasterly wind that can reach speeds of up to 124 miles per hour (200 km per hour), causing damage on land and disruption in sea transport. The gentle *yugo* blows from the south and is welcomed for the rain it brings to the plains. The *mistral* is a mild summer breeze that blows from the sea to the land and cools the hotter inland days. The *zgorac* blows from the land toward the sea.

RIVERS

The significant rivers in Croatia are the Sava, Drava, and Neretva rivers. Three-quarters of the Sava's 584 miles (940 km), not counting numerous tributaries, are within Croatia's boundaries. The capital city of Zagreb is built on the banks of the Sava. The Drava makes a third of its 465-mile (750-km) journey through Croatia. The Neretva, while a more modest 150 miles (240 km) long, provides the largest flow of water from Croatia into the Adriatic Sea. Only 30% of Croatia's rivers flow into the Adriatic; 70% terminate outside Croatia's control in the Black Sea—a fact that facilitated communications with Turkey in the past.

Of the three major rivers, only the Sava is navigable throughout its course. Some rivers are only navigable in part because of high waterfalls. In the 19th and early 20th centuries, when rivers were used to transport goods and deploy armed forces, these waterfalls were considered a nuisance. Today the rivers and waterfalls are a welcome source of hydroelectric energy.

The Neretva River originates in Bosnia and Herzegovina and cuts through the Dinaric Alps.

15

CITIES

Croatia has a longstanding urban culture. Despite a comparatively low population density of 215 people per square mile (83 people per square km), towns are more numerous in Croatia than in any other similarly sized area in southeastern Europe.

Most of these towns were founded in ancient or medieval times. Croatia's Roman ruins include an amphitheater in Pula (one of the world's best-preserved) and in Split, the monumental third century palace of Roman emperor Diocletian, which is recognized as the finest surviving example of classical defensive architecture in Europe. In Poreč, the mosaics of the Euphrasius Basilica are excellent examples of sixth century Byzantine art; whereas the architectural style of Zagreb and Ston is Gothic. The Renaissance shaped the character of Pag, Šibenik, Hvar, Korčula, and Dubrovnik, while the Baroque period left its mark on Varaždin and Vukovar.

Most of Croatia's cities have survived invasion and centuries of warfare. Their historic buildings have been modernized to function in modern urban centers. The 16th century Sponza Palace in Dubrovnik, which was a Customs House, is now home to the State Archives.

Opposite: **Zagreb, the capital, is the oldest city in Croatia. It lies between the southern slopes of the Medvednica Mountains and the Sava River.**

CITIES UNDER FIRE

Cities in the line of fire during the 1991–95 hostilities included Dubrovnik as well as Vukovar and Osijek, the urban centers nearest Serbia. Dubrovnik was hit by some 2,000 shells in 1991 and 1992. Two-thirds of the 824 buildings in the old town were damaged. The cost of replacing the unique terra-cotta rooftiles and repairing the fine white limestone walls was estimated at more than US$10 million. Because of the importance of Dubrovnik to world heritage and Croatian tourism, restoration has been rapidly undertaken. Baroque-style Vukovar, which lies across the Danube River from Serbia, has not been so lucky. Over 1,700 people, including 1,000 civilians, died trying to defend the city from Serbian forces. Over the course of a long siege, the city was reduced to ruins and the cost of eventual reconstruction is put at US$2.5 billion.

HISTORY

THE EARLIEST KNOWN inhabitants of Croatia did not live in beautiful cities, and perhaps discouraged by the seemingly insurmountable Alpine mountains, avoided the attractions of the coast. Instead, they settled in the low hills and forests to the north of present-day Zagreb, near today's town of Krapina.

Lacking the tidy and artistic habits of later inhabitants, prehistoric Krapina Man cooked his meals by throwing them in the fire, and having eaten his fill, tossed the remains over his shoulder to lie wherever they happened to fall on the floor of his cave. It is thanks to these untidy habits that anthropologists have been able to build a clear, though controversial, picture of the way he lived—as hunter, gatherer, and possibly, as cannibal. This suggestion and the debate surrounding it, have made Croatia one of the places on earth most studied by scholars attempting to recreate the course of human evolution.

Left: **A reconstruction of the prehistoric Krapina Man.**

Opposite: **Croatians of all ages were involved in their country's fight for independence.**

The Vindija cave site that is located 34 miles (55 km) north of Zagreb. Excavations of the cave in the 1970s support the cannibal theory proposed by Dragutin Gorjanović.

PREHISTORY

Evidence of early human life in Croatia goes back some 100,000 years to the Paleolithic period. Bones and craniums of *Homo Crapiniensis*, or Krapina Man, were found in the caves of northern Croatia by the Croatian paleontologist Dragutin Gorjanović between 1899 and 1906. Based on his findings, Gorjanović argued that Krapina Man was cannibalistic, a theory that has since been strongly contested.

Following the pioneering finds of Gorjanović, settled agricultural and fishing communities have been the subject of extensive excavations at Vucedol, near Vukovar. There, as in other fertile places throughout Europe, a permanent culture was established around 6000 B.C. Villages grew to a size similar to farming communities today, and people moved out of caves to construct permanent dwellings nearer their land. Animals were domesticated, and ceramic pots were made, glazed, and decorated with geometric designs. This Vucedol culture lasted from the late Stone Age to the Bronze Age (3000 B.C. to 2000 B.C.).

ENTER THE CROATS

Krapina Man was not the forefather of modern Croatians. Early Croatians were migrants from the east whose homeland is now southern Afghanistan and eastern Iran.

The first settlers in Croatia were the Illyrians, an Indo-European people who migrated from the east, probably around 1000 B.C. The Illyrians had a warlike reputation. Over a long period of time, they successfully resisted Greek encroachments from Macedonia and from the Adriatic coast and islands. Around 400 B.C. the Illyrians were driven out of Croatia by the Celts and Romans to what is now Albania.

The Romans invaded the Balkan peninsula in 300 B.C. and eventually controlled the entire area. They brought peace to the Baltic states, as they did to most of Europe, integrating all the lands they occupied into the Roman Empire in A.D. 10. In A.D. 395 the Roman Empire was divided into two. According to which half of the Drina River they were located on, Balkan states either belonged to the Western Roman Empire or the Byzantine Empire. Croatia was part of the Western Roman Empire, but on the empire's easternmost edge, its most vulnerable area.

At this time Croats, Serbs, and other Slavic tribes were living in a vast swampy terrain north and east of present-day Hungary, where they engaged in intermittent conflict with the Avars, who occupied much of the Hungarian plains. The Avars had ambitions of expanding their own fledgling empire at the expense of a weakened Roman Empire and were at this time launching regular attacks into Byzantium.

A Roman tablet found in the vaults of the Roman amphitheater in Pula.

A statue of Tomislav, the first Croatian king. His territory included all of present-day Croatia, part of Bosnia and Herzegovina, and the Montenegro coast.

THE NEW HOMELAND

Roman Emperor Heraclius (A.D. 610–641) offered the Croats land on the eastern shore of the Adriatic Sea if they would liberate that and other areas from the Avars, who were a constant headache to the empire. The Croats did such a good job that the Avars were never heard of again. Claiming their reward, the Croats settled throughout most of present-day Croatia and much of present-day Bosnia and Herzegovina and Serbia by the beginning of the seventh century. Croatia was born as a state but remained more a state of mind than a political entity. Its first action was to acknowledge the suzerainty of more powerful neighbors on both sides of the Western-Byzantium divide.

By 925 Croatia was independent. King Tomislav was crowned after he had successfully beaten back Magyar (Hungarian) attacks in the north and joined the Serbs to stand against the invading Bulgarians. Pope John X sent the crown to Tomislav with the message: "To my dear son Tomislav, King of the Croatians."

BETWEEN EAST AND WEST

In 1102 Croatia came under Hungarian control. By the 15th century Venice controlled the Dalmatian coast, and Turkey ruled those parts of Croatia not seized by Venice. In 1526 after the death of Hungarian King Ludovik II, the Hapsburgs of Austria claimed the Hungarian throne. The Croatian *Sabor* ("SAH-bor"), or parliament, made Archduke Ferdinand of Austria the king of Croatia so that he would help fight the Turks. At the end of the 17th century, Turkey finally renounced all claims to Croatia.

Austrian control was briefly interrupted in 1805 when Napoleon Bonaparte beat the Austrian and Prussian forces at Austerlitz and took the Dalmatian coast as one of his prizes. The fall of the Napoleonic empire in 1815 led to the Congress of Vienna, which recognized Austria's claim to Dalmatia, while placing the rest of Croatia under the jurisdiction of Hungary.

Austria gave Dalmatia back to its former master, Venice, and Hungary immediately sought to "culturally cleanse" Croatia. In 1815 Hungarian language and culture were imposed throughout Croatia. Opposition to this was led by a group that called itself the Croatian Illyrian Movement. As opposition grew, an attempt was made to defuse the situation. In 1867 the Croatians were given their own parliament and the right to use the Croatian language, but Croatia was still subordinate to Hungary. While most Croatian opposition remained nonviolent, an armed rebellion broke out in 1871. Even though it failed, it gave the Hapsburgs the excuse to expand their control over the whole of Bosnia and Herzegovina.

The Turks built this skull tower in Nĭs, southeastern Serbia, from the skulls of their enemies.

YUGOSLAVIA

The Kingdom of
Serbs, Croats, and
Slovenes was a
creation destined
for disaster,
because it con-
sisted of diverse
ethnic groups,
traditions, lan-
guages, and
religions. When
the Serbs gained
ascendancy in the
government,
suspicion arose
among the Croats
that the kingdom
(and later, its
successor, Yugo-
slavia) was part of
a plan to create a
"Greater Serbia."

On December 1, 1918, as part of the post World War I European settlement, the Kingdom of Serbs, Croats, and Slovenes was formed, headed by the prince regent (later king) Aleksandar. Soon, differences appeared between Croats and Serbs, and these erupted into armed hostilities in the 1920s. To suppress the violence, King Aleksandar imposed direct rule in 1929 and renamed the country "Yugoslavia." His move was opposed by a group of young Croatians and Macedonians, who assassinated him in 1934.

When World War II broke out, Yugoslavia was disunited and easily taken by German and Italian troops. The Independent State of Croatia was proclaimed in April 1941 under a German puppet administration called the *Ustaše*, which set up a brutal program to cleanse Croatia of Serbs, Gypsies, and Jews. Not all Croats supported the *Ustaše*. Many joined the Serbs and united under Josip Broz Tito in armed resistance.

With the end of World War II in 1945, the dream of Yugoslavia again became a reality, this time under the control of antifascist forces led by Tito. Until his death in 1980, Tito controlled Yugoslavia and steered the Yugoslav Communist Party along a uniquely neutral path between the Soviet bloc and the Western North Atlantic Treaty Organization alliance.

For the next few decades, Serbs and Croats appeared to have buried their differences. In 1971, however, resentment at the redistribution of Croatia's wealth to the poorer republics in the federation led to a "Croatian Spring" when reformers called for greater economic autonomy. They were jailed or removed from positions of influence. In 1974, when the threat from Croatia had abated, the republics were given more autonomy. The stage was thus set for the conflict between republics that followed the disintegration of communism in Europe in the late 1980s. It led to the breakup of the Socialist Republic of Yugoslavia.

JOSIP BROZ TITO

Born Josip Broz in Kumrovec, northwest of Zagreb, in 1892, the son of a Croat father and a Slovene mother, Tito was drafted into the German army during World War I and taken prisoner by the Russians. He escaped and joined the Red Army in 1917, fighting to help establish the Soviet Union. He returned to Croatia in 1920 and, as secretary of the outlawed Communist Party, worked for two decades to increase party membership.

As a result of his communist activities, he was arrested in 1928 and imprisoned for five years. After his release in 1934, he adopted the pseudonym, Tito. When the Germans invaded Yugoslavia in 1941, Tito led a national resistance movement. His campaign of resistance was supported militarily by Britain and the United States but not by the Soviet Union.

In 1945 Tito became premier of Yugoslavia. He clashed with Stalin and in 1948 was dismissed from the Cominform, which was an organization set up to share information among European communist parties. For the rest of his life, Tito walked a tightrope between East and West and was preoccupied with holding together the ethnic groups of Yugoslavia in what has been called a "balance of powers federation."

Using stick and carrot, Tito managed to unite Serbs, Croats, ethnic Albanians, Slovenes, and Macedonians for 35 years. Under his astute leadership, Croatia prospered, building huge tourist and shipbuilding industries, and a little petrochemical empire.

When Tito died in May 1980, the population of Yugoslavia mourned him sincerely. For 10 years after his death, the country was beset by economic problems, ethnic violence, and rival nationalisms that eventually led to the destruction of Tito's Yugoslavia.

Tito took his name after Tito Brezovački, an 18th century Croat writer.

Above: **The Croatian parliament is sworn in after the country declared independence from Yugoslavia.**

Opposite: **A British U.N. soldier monitors a group of Croat refugees.**

AN INDEPENDENT CROATIA

As communism fell apart in Eastern Europe, the six republics and two autonomous provinces that made up the Yugoslav federation began to reassert their individual identities. In May 1990 the Croatian Democratic Union (HDZ), headed by Franjo Tudjman, won the Croatian elections. In a referendum a year later, 93% of the population of Croatia voted in favor of independence. Following this clear mandate, Croatia declared independence on June 25, 1991.

THE 1991–95 HOSTILITIES

After Croatia declared independence, there was a mass dismissal of the 600,000-strong Serb community from public service. Krajina, a predominantly Serb area that is in the Šibenik-Knin region, declared its independence from Croatia. Following inter-ethnic violence and armed intervention from Serbia in support of the Serbs in Croatia, the European Union advised Croatia to freeze its declaration of independence for three months to avoid further bloodshed.

Meanwhile, the fighting intensified and spread, and on October 7, 1991, the presidential palace in Zagreb was hit by rockets in a Serb attempt to kill President Tudjman. On October 8, 1991, when the moratorium on independence expired, Croatia declared itself a republic. Thus, there are three dates in 1991 relating to Croatia's independence: the May referendum, the declaration of independence on June 25, and the declaration on October 8. Croatia has settled on May 30 to celebrate its status of independent statehood. Croatia's independence was recognized by the European Union and 100 other countries. It was admitted to the United Nations in 1992.

In December 1995 the Dayton Peace Agreement for the former Yugoslavia confirmed Croatian control within the current boundaries of the country. In the 1997 elections Tudjman and the Croatian Democratic Union were returned to power.

GOVERNMENT

FROM 1945 TO 1991 Croatia's identity was subsumed within the identity of the former Socialist Federal Republic of Yugoslavia, and Croatia was controlled by the Communist Party from the capital, Belgrade, in Serbia. Since 1991 the new, noncommunist government has set out to create a truly independent Croatia, while attempting to guarantee freedom for Serbs, Muslims, and other minorities.

Article 115 of the December 22, 1990 constitution defines Croatia as an indivisible, democratic, and social state structured on the separation of executive, judicial, and legislative powers. The president is head of state and commander of the armed forces. He is elected by popular vote for five years, renewable for another five-year period of office.

The constitution also stipulates that the prime minister and the deputy prime minister are directly appointed by the president, as are several members of parliament.

Left: **The National Assembly building in Markov Square in Zagreb.**

Opposite: **The changing of the guard outside the Presidential Palace.**

LOCAL GOVERNMENT

Croatia is divided into 21 *županijas* ("zhoo-PAH-nee-yahs"), or regional counties. There are two self-governing *kotari* ("ko-TAH-ree"), or districts, Glina and Knin, which are under local Serb control. County boundaries are designed to reflect local, historic, and economic considerations.

Županijas were introduced in the 10th century as a more advanced form of structuring the Croatian state. In the 1990 constitution, they were reintroduced, and two years later the Croatian parliament passed a law to determine the boundaries of the counties, towns, and municipalities. Each county acts with a great measure of autonomy in matters of local administration and local government. Similarly, the 416 municipalities and 122 town councils in Croatia are largely self-governing.

THE LEGISLATURE

Croatia has a two-house legislature, the *Sabor*, which loosely resembles that of the United States. The two houses are *Zupanijski Dom* ("zoo-PAH-neey-skee DOM"), which can be translated as the House of Districts or the Chamber of Counties, and the *Zastupnički Dom* ("ZAH-stoop-neech-kee DOM"), translated variously as the House of Representatives or the Chamber of Deputies. The members of both houses serve four-year terms.

The House of Districts introduces, debates, and puts forward motions for consideration by the House of Representatives. Of the 68 seats in the House of Districts, five are directly appointed by the president and 63 are elected by popular vote.

The House of Representatives passes laws, proposes constitutional reform, adopts the national budget, and decides on matters of defense and sovereignty. There are 127 seats in the House of Representatives, 12 of

The 21 counties in Croatia are Bjelovar-Bilogora, City of Zagreb, Dubrovnik-Neretva, Istra, Karlovac, Koprivnica-Krizevci, Krapina-Zagorje, Lika-Senj, Medimurje, Osijek-Baranja, Pozega-Slavonia, Primorje-Gorski Kotar, Šibenik, Sisak-Moslavina, Slavonski Brod-Posavina, Split-Dalmatia, Varaždin, Virovitica-Podravina, Vukovar-Srijem, Zadar-Knin, and Zagreb.

which are for members elected by the proportional vote of Croatian
citizens living overseas, and seven for members of national minorities
elected from a special list of candidates. Thus, the electoral system of
"adjusted proportional representation" is designed to ensure that minorities
have a voice in the House, and that the many overseas Croatians who
helped financially in the fight for independence are not forgotten.

THE JUDICIARY

The highest judicial authority in Croatia, as in the United States, is the
Supreme Court, to which appeals against decisions by county courts may
be made. Judges are appointed for eight-year terms by the State Judicial
Council of the Republic, which is elected by the House of Representatives.

Questions relating to the constitution are referred to the Constitutional
Court, whose 11 judges are also elected by the State Judicial Council of the
Republic. They sit for eight-year terms.

FOUNDER OF INDEPENDENT CROATIA

The founder and first president of the Republic of Croatia, Franjo Tudjman, was born on May 14, 1922, in Veliko Trgovisce, northwest Croatia. At the age of 19, he joined the antifascist partisan movement to fight against the *Ustaše* regime. In 1960 Tudjman became the youngest general in the Yugoslav army. Two years later he left the military to study history and eventually headed the Institute for the History of the Workers' Movement. Tudjman was kicked out of the Communist Party in 1967 for questioning the number of *Ustaše* victims. In the early 1970s he was jailed for three years for being a part of a movement to get more independence for Croatia.

President Franjo Tudjman at an international conference.

In February 1981, for speaking against the communist system during interviews with journalists from Swedish and German television and French radio, Tudjman was sentenced to a three-year prison term and prohibited from engaging in public activity for a further five years. In 1989 Tudjman founded the Hrvatska Demokratska Zajednica (HDZ), or Croatian Democratic Union, and became its president. After his party's victory in the first Croatian democratic elections, he was elected president in 1990. He was reelected in the presidential elections of June 1997.

Tudjman's popularity declined in later years. Since he came to power, Croatians have become poorer, and unemployment hit an all-time high of 20.8% in December 1999. His government was accused of corruption, cronyism, and inefficiency, and the Croatian political system was described as "nominally democratic." Tudjman's nationalistic beliefs, which won him the presidency in 1990, implemented policies that fueled a civil war with Serbs in Croatia. The 1991–95 hostilities resulted in the loss of 250,000 lives, and the economy suffered.

In a decade as president of Croatia, Tudjman imposed a one-man rule, which means he had the final say in parliamentary and judicial matters. Tudjman's near-dictatorial rule ended on December 10, 1999, with his death after an illness.

The opposition coalition that defeated the ruling party in 2000 is made up of the Social Democratic Party, led by Ivica Račan, and the Croatian Social Liberal Party, led by Dražen Budiša. Račan is now the prime minister of Croatia.

PARLIAMENTARY ELECTIONS

After the death of Franjo Tudjman, parliamentary elections were held on January 3, 2000. The ruling party, the nationalistic Croatian Democratic Union, was ousted from power. Croatians voted in favor of a center-left alliance made up of a six-party coalition. The new government promised democratic reform and that it would work toward joining the European Union (EU) and the North Atlantic Treaty Organization (NATO).

A man casting his vote during the January 2000 presidential elections.

PRESIDENTIAL ELECTIONS

Croatia's presidential elections were held on January 24, 2000. Nine candidates were fielded, but two men took the lead. Stipe Mesić, a lawyer, gathered 41% of the vote, while Dražen Budiša, a former communist dissident, collected 28%. As there was no clear majority, a runoff election was held on February 7. This time, Stipe Mesić emerged victorious with 56.21% of the vote.

CURRENT LEADER

Sixty-five-year-old Stipe Mesić was a deputy in the Croatian parliament in the 1960s. He was imprisoned in 1972 for two years for promoting Croatian nationalism. In the 1990s Mesić represented Croatia in the Yugoslav presidency. On July 30, 1991, after Croatia's declaration of independence, he became the last president of the former Yugoslavia at the suggestion of European and United States officials.

Mesić joined Tudjman's Croatian Democratic Union to participate in the fight for Croatia's independence. He left in 1994 after expressing his disapproval of the corruption and authoritarianism that were present in the party.

Many Croatians regard Mesić as a war hero for the crucial role he played in the Serbia-Croatia hostilities from 1991 to 1995. For instance, when the Yugoslav army shelled Dubrovnik, Mesić led a fleet of small boats along the Adriatic coast to draw the world's attention to the bombardment.

A triumphant Stipe Mesić after winning the Croatian presidency in February 2000.

ECONOMY

CROATIA'S GEOGRAPHIC LOCATION has greatly influenced its economy. Inland, the Pannonian Plain supports industry and agriculture, while on the coast there are ports, and tourism and fishing industries. Unfortunately in the 1990s, the war with Serbia and conflicts between Croatia's neighbors greatly reduced tourism and investment and have led to high unemployment and declining real wages.

Against this difficult economic backdrop, the government established a ministry of privatization to propose changes in the laws. Initially, employees and former employees of government-owned companies have the opportunity to purchase company shares under favorable conditions. Eventually, large industrial enterprises, hotels, and public companies such as telecommunications and energy providers will be privatized. Foreign investment is welcomed and treated like domestic investment, except that foreigners have the guaranteed right to transfer and repatriate profits.

Left: **A factory manufacturing food products.**

Opposite: **Craftsmen repairing a tiled roof in Dubrovnik, which was destroyed in the war with Serbia. Since the war, building and construction have become major industries in Croatia.**

A textile factory.

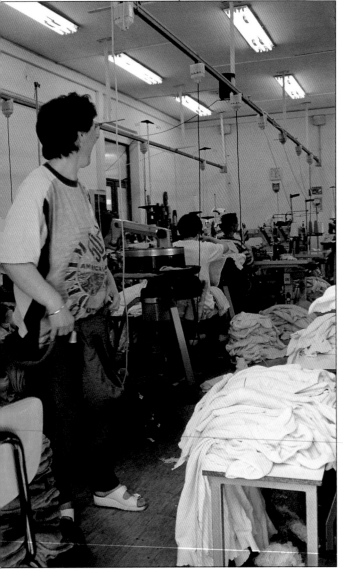

SIGNIFICANT SOURCES OF REVENUE

Before the breakup of Yugoslavia, Croatia was the world's third largest shipbuilder. Other major industries were chemicals, machine-tool manufacturing, heavy electrical engineering, textiles, and tourism, which contributed one-third of Croatia's national income. Also significant were the oil and gas industry, food processing, leather, furniture, and wood products.

After peace was restored in 1995, Croatia became badly indebted—estimates of damages caused by the war have exceeded US$7 billion, the total value of goods exported at the turn of the 21st century was less than half that of goods imported, and Croatia's biggest revenue earner, tourism, declined dramatically. From providing a third of the national income, tourist revenues fell to almost zero. Attempts made to help the tourist industry in 1998–99 were dashed by the war in Kosovo.

According to the conditions of the Dayton Plan, measures to revive the economy must take second place to humanitarian consider-ations. The immediate priority is the return of refugees, mostly Serbs (including those who fled in fear and those who were physically expelled) to their homes.

CROATIAN SHIPBUILDING

Croatia, far from the world's shipping lanes, was the third biggest shipbuilder in the world in the 1960s. Only Japan and Korea produced more and bigger ships.

Croatia has one of the longest traditions of shipbuilding in the world, stretching back over one thousand years. The only interruption came during the 16th to 18th centuries when Venetian rule in Dalmatia forbade Croatian construction of ships and denuded Croatia's coastal timber to support Venice's own shipbuilding industry.

During the 1960s and 1970s, Croatia constructed ships in excess of 200,000 tons for demanding clients, mostly in the United States and Scandinavia. While the global economic recession of the late 1990s and Croatia's economic difficulties will cause problems for the reconstruction of this industry, the Croatian Shipbuilders Association hopes to maximize the capacity of Croatia's shipyards by matching the productivity of Japan and Korea in a few years. This goal was given encouragement when Great Britain's Royal Shipbuilding Institute declared a petroleum and chemicals tanker built in Croatia's Trogir shipyard to be the best ship built anywhere in the world in 1998.

Croatia's major trading partners, in order of importance, are Italy, Germany, Bosnia and Herzegovina, Slovenia, Austria, and Russia.

Peasants plowing their field in the fertile Pannonian Plain.

PRIMARY OCCUPATIONS AND INDUSTRIES

With the exception of a few large collective farms, agriculture was the only economic sector left in private hands during the 45 years of communist rule. Today 82% of cultivated land is privately owned, and farmers continue to work their small plots.

Construction has, for many years, been a stable industry in Croatia. From the 1960s to the 1980s this sector grew, building hotels and other tourist-related facilities. However, construction almost stopped during the 1991–95 war. Since then, the building industry has revived, with the need for national reconstruction, including the reconstruction of heritage sites supported by international donations. In 1997 construction work in Croatia employed 58,037 people, making the industry a top employer. Thanks to the skills and the relatively low cost of Croatian workers, an increasing number of international competitive contracts are being won by Croatia. In 1997 construction contracts carried out abroad amounted to more than US$154 million, 95% of which was earned in Europe.

AGRICULTURE AND FORESTRY

Agriculture in Croatia is well developed. There are 7.4 million acres (three million hectares) of agricultural land of which 61.3% is cultivated. The remainder is pasture land. Most of the cultivated area is found within the fertile Pannonian region, which covers some 55% of the country's total surface area and produces most of its food and farm products.

Of Croatia's extensive forests, 76% are state-owned, with the rest in private hands. The rich resource of high quality timber has fed a growing wood-processing and furniture industry that employs 40,000 workers and generates US$350 million in export income. As forest resources decline in the rest of the world, Croatia's relatively cheap and plentiful hardwoods are very attractive to the United States and northern Europe. The Croatian common oak, renowned for its beautiful color and hardness, is in great demand when made into solid period furniture and high quality parquet— such products are almost totally exported and bring in badly needed US dollars and Deutschemarks.

Market stalls selling wood and wicker products are easily found in Croatia.

41

Souvenirs and trinkets for sale in Korčula, the sixth largest island in Croatia.

TOURISM

Until 1990 tourism was Croatia's largest source of foreign currency and a major source of employment. The 1991–95 war brought about a sudden end to the tourist boom and to a major industry.

Although Croatia has been at peace since 1995, hostilities in neighboring Balkan countries have not helped attempts to regenerate tourism. By the mid 1990s tourist arrivals fell dramatically compared to that in the 1980s.

From 1995 to 1998 tourism slowly increased but never accounted for more than 4% of Gross National Product (GNP), compared to industry and mining at 30% and agriculture and fishing at 12%.

In 1999 the NATO bombing of Serbia caused tourism in Croatia to nosedive again, with newly renovated hotels left empty and newly trained staff redundant before they had even begun work.

The war over Kosovo gave a short-term boost to the oil and gas industry, with Croatia supplying oil to its former enemy as fast as NATO could bomb Serbia's fuel supplies. But this in no way made up for the money lost by the dislocation of Croatia's plans to revive tourism to its former glory by the year 2000.

Growing mushrooms in the dark.

TRUFFLES

Croatia's plans for an overall economic revival are based on a transition from state control to one of individual initiative. Curiously, the most talked-about export in 1999, both legal and illegal, was a small and rather shrivelled mushroom—the truffle.

Truffles are said by the Croatians to be the most delicious mushrooms in the world and are surrounded with a mystical folklore lauding their aphrodisiac qualities. They are not cultivated but are found wild in the forests, most abundantly in the Istria region.

Croatians have bred and trained some 12,000 special truffle-hunting dogs called *breks* ("BREKS") to sniff out the prized mushrooms during the short three-month truffle season from October to January. France, Italy, and Spain are the traditional truffle producers and consumers, but Croatian truffles are said to be tastier and cost half the price of those sold by their more experienced counterparts.

How much truffles contribute to the economy is not known, since much of the harvest is smuggled to Italy, where at least part is sold under Italian labels. Thousands of Croatians are said to have joined the great truffle hunt in 1999, hoping for extra income.

OVER-CROPPING

Fish and shellfish exports increased toward the end of the 20th century, raising concerns that Croatia was overfishing the Adriatic Sea. Timber exports are also on the increase, and similar cautions are beginning to be heard in the forest products industry.

There have been suggestions that Croatia is trying to buy its way out of a difficult economic period through over-exploitation of its resources. Unfortunately for those intent on decentralizing the economy, the overenthusiastic removal of government control of fisheries and forest industries opens the possibility of inappropriate exploitation by individuals trying to get rich or overcome poverty. At the end of the 20th century, accusations of corruption and profiteering were made against some of the politicians elected to place Croatia's national interests first.

An oyster farmer sorting out shellfish in his boat.

ENERGY SOURCES

As people and industry became poorer after 1991, the consumption of energy decreased. This led to a small increase in the export of energy, mostly in the form of liquid fuel and natural gas by pipeline to Serbia, Bosnia and Herzegovina, and Slovenia.

Croatia is fortunate in having a relative abundance of oil and natural gas. Nevertheless, domestic sources provided only 30% of Croatia's needs during economic good times, and it was necessary to import the shortfall. Plans exist to expand the use of oil and gas and for greater exploitation of these resources.

The Croatian petrochemical industry is established on the island of Krk, an ideal entry point for crude oil, gas, and petroleum products that are bound for Central and East European countries. This is largely because of the qualities of Krk's deep-water port and its proximity to Central Europe. Prospects for developing both the domestic energy sector and the entrepot trade in energy for re-export are bright.

A Croatian worker climbs over pipelines in Sisak. The refinery here was destroyed by Yugoslav shelling.

WORKING LIFE

The average wage of Croatians was US$624 a month in November 1997. Although this figure is not low in terms of the surrounding Balkan states, it is among the lowest in Europe. The national currency, the kuna, is tied to the Deutschemark, and inflation is in keeping with European figures at 3.6%. An unemployment rate of 20.8% (December 1999 figure), one of the highest in Europe, is a major problem which affects the individual wealth of families and the country's attempts to improve the economy.

The addition of a high indirect taxation rate—a value-added tax of 22% was introduced in 1997—has done nothing to help workers and families. The cost of a meal in a self-service restaurant, 25 kuna (US$4), and the average intercity bus fare, 45 kuna (US$7.50), give an idea of how family budgets must be managed to provide the basics of life.

Right: **The kuna replaced the Croatian dinar as the national currency in May 1994. The kuna, or marten, is an animal found in Croatia. Its pelt was an acceptable means of exchange in the Middle Ages. The kuna is divided into 100 lipa.**

Opposite: **People waiting to board a bus in Split.**

INFRASTRUCTURE

Croatia's economic infrastructure is below the standard of developed European countries. The country has 18,009 miles (29,000 km) of roads, of which 12,420 miles (20,000 km) are paved, and 1,717 miles (2,763 km) of railroad track, of which 611 miles (983 km) are electrified. The main ports of Rijeka, Split, and Ploče are well connected to the interior. Currently, construction of 1,242 additional miles (2,000 km) of roads and 310 miles (500 km) of track is under way, financed primarily by foreign loans and concessions.

River transport is generally less important than in the past, except on Croatia's major river, the Sava, which is the subject of an international plan to link the Danube and Sava rivers and construct an inland port at the Croatian city of Osijek.

Despite the poor economic situation, postal and telephone services have greatly improved in recent years. Long-distance buses are also run efficiently and frequently.

Croatia's transport network has stronger links to Europe than to the Balkans: two trains connect Zagreb and Belgrade every day, and four trains run daily between the two capitals, Zagreb and Budapest.

CROATIANS

THE CROATIAN WAR of independence and similar conflicts in neighboring states caused a great movement of people across new national boundaries. Generally, such movement was inspired by fear and involved people moving from an area where they were an ethnic minority to an area where they were the majority. With peace, a reverse movement has taken place. But not everybody has gone—or is expected to go—home. Thus, reliable statistics on population and ethnicity are difficult to find and compile.

ETHNIC GROUPS

Before 1990, 78% of Croatians were ethnic Croat, that is, they saw themselves as Croat, spoke Croatian, and most followed the beliefs of the Roman Catholic Church and shared a common view of history and origin. About 12% of Croatians were ethnic Serbs, but many left Croatia during the violence. Some have moved back to Croatia since, but it is likely the Serb community will remain smaller than its prewar size.

Other groups in Croatia include small communities of Slavic Muslims, Hungarians, Slovenes, Italians, Czechs, Albanians, and Jews. The new constitution and legislative structure attempt to ensure that such groups are proportionately represented in the House of Representatives. Their rights are constitutionally guaranteed under the final settlements that ended the hostilities of the 1990s.

Officially, there are about 4.7 million Croatians, both Croats and minorities, living in Croatia. An estimated one million ethnic Croats live in other states in the former Yugoslavia, especially in Bosnia and Herzegovina. Another 2.3 million Croats live elsewhere overseas.

Above: **Young Croatians sitting in a main square in Zagreb.**

Opposite: **A Croatian child displays the relaxed, easygoing demeanor of Croatians.**

After the fall of Vukovar to the federal Yugoslav forces in 1991, it was estimated that 15,000 people out of a population of 50,000 fled the city.

THE CROATIAN DIASPORA

Of the ethnic Croats living overseas, 1.5 million are in the United States, 270,000 in Germany, 240,000 in Australia, 150,000 in Canada, and another 150,000 in Argentina. Overseas Croatians may retain their citizenship, unless they renounce it, and may vote for members of the House of Representatives from a special list internationally distributed.

The Croatian diaspora has a long history. In the 14th and 15th centuries many young men left Croatia to pursue higher education in Italy and elsewhere. Some returned, many did not. When the Turks invaded Croatia in the 15th century, some 400,000 Croatians left for Italy, Austria, Hungary, Slovakia, and Romania. Wherever they went, they preserved their language, customs, and culture. In the southern Italian province of Molise, a group of wholly Croatian villages may be found.

The Croatian Diaspora

Croatians were also among the earliest settlers in the New World with communities in Canada, the southern United States, and Mexico. Names on tombstones beside the Savannah River in Georgia show that a community of over 1,200 Croatians were massacred during the American Civil War (1861–65). Today in Canada, thousands of Croatians dressed in national costume gather each year to celebrate the Canadian Croatian Folklore Festival.

The diaspora was fueled by problems at home and attractions overseas. Following the example of Croatian Christian leaders who fled the Turks and prospered in Europe, Croatian Muslims later fled the Austro-Hungarian empire and moved to Turkey where they were welcomed. From 1900 to 1914 emigration from Croatia was so massive that it was predicted that Croatia would not survive as a nation. Between World War I and World War II, Croatia remained divided and poor. At that time, some 100,000 Croatians were attracted to the opportunities in South America and the mines of Belgium.

Even after World War II, emigration continued with the blessing of the communist authorities because it reduced unemployment at home, eased political pressure, and was the major source of hard currency for the new country. About 800,000 Croatians left to work in other European countries at this time. Most never returned, and many joined in secondary migration to Australia, Canada, and the United States. Their dollars were sent to relatives in Croatia and helped to build the economy, including one of the largest tourist industries in the world.

A custom has developed for emigrants to take some ancestral soil with them and, when the time comes, to be buried with it. This inspired Croat poet Drago Ivanišević to write, "As a Croat I am brother of all men. Wherever I go Croatia is with me."

Almost half of the Croatian population lives outside Croatia, having left for economic rather than political reasons. In the late 19th century, they were often called on to support refugees, some of whom had crossed the borders illegally. In the 20th century, these overseas Croatians contributed significantly to the war fund in their homeland.

A traditional village house made entirely of stone. Houses like these are only found in rural areas.

SOCIAL HIERARCHIES

Like other Europeans, Croatians are susceptible to the divisions and injustices created by the growth of social hierarchy in their society. In the past, the peasant classes lived in small stone houses, which blended into the land on which they worked, and the aristocracy lived in castles that towered toward the heavens.

Back then, the Croatians were also divided linguistically; only the peasants and working classes spoke Croat. The upper classes associated themselves with the occupying powers, to the point of speaking Hungarian or German as their first language. The Illyrian movement that started in the 1830s was ostensibly for the revival of the Croatian language; by its nature the movement appealed to the Croat-speaking masses and targeted the upper classes.

Generally, aristocracies like to maintain their social position and material possessions over time, passing them down through the generations. However, Croatian aristocrats never managed to entrench their position to the same extent as their European counterparts. Their hold over their subjects was always tenuous. In the 20th century, the Croats and Serbs, who speak the same language, came together to take control of parts of Slavonia and Dalmatia under local Serbo-Croatian-speaking governments. They were often as opposed to their homegrown rulers as to foreign powers. Thus, the idea of a united Yugoslavia originated at the bottom of the social hierarchy.

A Croatian peasant sitting on a wagon.

THE FREE PEASANTS

Intent on forming a buffer against the advancing Turks in the 16th century, the Hapsburgs were happy to allow a gypsy-like group of nomads, known as Vlachs, to settle on the marshy land south of Zagreb.

The settlers appear to have been a Slav clan like the Croats and Serbs. They spoke a Slavic language readily intelligible to Croats but belonged to the Orthodox Church. In addition, they remained outside of the harsh feudal system that the Hapsburgs introduced, and which the Croatian nobility implemented.

The Hapsburgs allowed the Vlachs to remain free, landowning peasants, reasoning that they would better defend their own land than the land of a feudal lord. The rationale was sound. The free peasants not only made good soldiers against the Turks, they defended their land against everybody who tried to dispossess them, including the Croatian nobility and the *Sabor*, which repeatedly failed to turn them into serfs.

The free peasants maintained their rights throughout the communist years and lost them only when, having sided with the Serbs during the war, they were expelled from Croatia in 1995.

Even though most Croatians wear Western-style clothes, they will keep a spotless folk costume in a bottom drawer, to be taken out and worn for festivals.

COSTUME

The character of Croatia's many regions is reflected in their traditional folk costumes. The most colorful and finely embroidered clothing is found in the rich and fertile Pannonian plain. In the more rugged Alpine region, both male and female costumes are simpler, often woven from rough, homemade white cloth. On the Dalmatian coast, the traditional dress reflects the mild climate. Today folk costume is reserved for holidays and special occasions.

Folk costumes and activities were promoted by Tito as a solution to national and ethnic sectarianism, and as an alternative form of social identity and social activity to the Church. Following in Tito's footsteps, President Tudjman promoted folk activities and made use of folk motifs. The political attention to elements of folklore in the culture has not only preserved the costumes, traditions, and artifacts of folklore, but has assisted Croatia in maintaining the spirit of folklore—the harmony of people and their environment.

SOME FAMOUS CROATIANS

ANDRIJA MOHOROVIČIĆ (1857–1936) This meteorologist and geophysicist was born in Volosko (one mile east of Opatija town), son of a shipyard carpenter. Mohorovičić discovered the Moho-layer, essential for understanding the structure of the earth and the behavior of seismic waves. Later he came up with a method of locating earthquake epicenters and calculating the velocity of seismic waves.

NIKOLA TESLA (1856–1943) Nikola Tesla was of Serbian origin, son of an Orthodox priest. He studied electrical engineering at the University of Prague. In 1884 Tesla migrated to the United States and arrived in New York with a few cents in his pocket. He found work with Thomas Edison but they soon parted company because of their incompatible personalities. Tesla developed the first system of generating and transmitting alternating current for electric power and sold the rights to Westinghouse in 1885. Six years later, he invented the Tesla coil that became widely used in radio and television sets. The scientific unit for measuring magnetic induction, the tesla, is named after him.

MARCO POLO (1253–1324) This internationally known traveler and explorer is often thought of as Venetian, but Croatian historians claim that he was born on the island of Korčula in Dalmatia.

Left: **Croatia-born American physicist and electrical engineer, Nikola Tesla.**

Right: **Marco Polo, explorer and merchant.**

LIFESTYLE

A GREAT MAJORITY of Croatians consider themselves devout Catholics, European rather than Balkan, and unequivocally on the right side in the confrontation between Serbs and Croats. This view of the world and a Croat's place in it corresponds to Croatia's formative history.

Croatia has long pictured itself as the last outpost of the civilized, Western and Christian world. This idea began when the Romans divided their empire into west and east in A.D. 395. Croatia, Slovenia, and Bosnia became part of the Western Roman Empire, and Serbia and Macedonia were included in the Byzantine Empire.

Although these events took place several centuries before today's Croatians appeared in Croatia, the sense of hanging on the edge of civilization, whether or not based on a relevant history, is a distinct trait of the Croatian personality.

Left: **Two girls and their father on the way to church. Croatians go to church regularly and include religion in all aspects of their lives.**

Opposite: **Children playing in the street without a care in the world.**

Boys selling shells and pieces of coral on Hvar Island to supplement their family's income.

ECONOMIC WOES

Croatians see no paradox in bemoaning the economic woes that plagued Croatia in the last decade of the 20th century and talking nostalgically of the comparative wealth of the 1970s and 1980s, when Croatia was part of communist Yugoslavia. If pushed to explain how this situation came about, Croatians blame the cost and disruptions of war, which in turn are blamed on the Serbs.

Economic problems are real for most Croatian families at the beginning of the 21st century. They have less money and must prioritize their spending. This is not immediately evident in the street however. Families may limit trips to the movies or the theater and forego the purchase of a car, but they are dressed stylishly, often in expensive clothes imported from Europe.

TABOOS AND TOLERANCE

Croatians take a tolerant and pragmatic view of life, rather than a dogmatic one, and their lifestyle contains few taboos. While the Catholic Church's views on birth control are known and respected, condoms are readily available and locally manufactured.

There is no taboo against nudity. At the end of the 20th century, more than 30 nudist areas, mostly on beaches and open to all, existed in Croatia. Outside of these areas, topless sunbathing will raise as few eyebrows in Croatia as it would in France or Germany.

Nightclubs and discos swing until 4.00 A.M. Homosexuality is tolerated as much as it is in the most progressive European countries.

A Western fast-food outlet in Zagreb.

TOWN AND COUNTRY

As everywhere, traditions are more evident in the rural village than in the urban city. Social interaction is more clearly formulated and meaningful in rural areas where people know their neighbors well and meet them every day, than in the city, where strangers pass on the street.

The model village is now found in only a few mountain areas. Croatia has for centuries been more urbanized than most parts of eastern Europe. Towns are, in general, medieval in style, with houses packed tightly behind defensive walls. Compared to towns in other industrialized countries, people living in Croatian towns feel less alienated, and identity with the town of one's origin is strong.

A woman milking her cow in a village in central Dalmatia.

THE LIFE CYCLE

While norms will differ between the majority Catholic and the minority Orthodox Christians, Muslims, and Jews, all Croatians attach great importance to the main life-cycle rites of birth, marriage, and death. All three events must be sanctioned by religious ritual.

The wedding feast is perhaps the most public and expensive rite. A family of modest means will do all within its power, even entering into debt, to provide a memorable wedding. This is particularly true in the countryside, where the entire village may be invited, or two villages if the marriage is cross-village. Even in the towns, a wedding provides an occasion for distant relatives to come together, and these relatives expect to be invited and feasted.

Weddings involve folk elements as well as church rituals. Today, it is usual to have a large church wedding followed by an even larger secular celebration, attended by friends and relatives.

A wedding party outside St. Mark's Church, Zagreb. Today's brides and bridegrooms may change attire during their wedding day, entering the church in formal Western wedding dress, then donning the folk costumes of their birthplace in the evening.

A Croatian family on a weekend outing.

THE FAMILY

The basic residential unit in Croatia is the nuclear family—a husband, wife, and three or four children. A widowed grandparent will often share the living quarters and have a close relationship with the children. Compared to families in the cities, those in rural areas are larger as extended familes live together.

In Croatia it is normal for the elderly to be cared for by their children or grandchildren. In farming communities, this is ensured because the land and house are likely to pass from father to son. Given the economic hardship after independence, and given the fact that old-age pensions of any substance are few and far between, this social function of the family is unlikely to change quickly in the future, even in the urban areas.

EDUCATION

Education in Croatia has a long history. Records from the 10th century show Tomislav, the first king of Croatia, exhorting his subjects to send their children to school so they might become learned monks and nuns. Several monastic centers of higher education led to the opening of what began as the first known Croatian university, founded in Zagreb by Jesuits in 1669. It mainly taught classical philology, law, philosophy, and theology.

Today there are four universities in Croatia: in Zagreb, Osijek, Rijeka, and Split. The quality of education, especially in science, medicine, and engineering, is said to meet the highest international standards.

Education is obligatory for eight years. While there are no school or university fees, few Croatians can spare the time to go to secondary school and university—many have to work to support their families.

Students at Zagreb University. About 5.3% of the population have a college degree.

HEALTH

The standard of medical care in Croatia meets international standards. However, costs are much higher than before independence. The Croatian work force has access to free medical care, but unemployed workers, who constituted 17.6% in 1999, often do not.

In general, the health situation is favorable. Compared to some other parts of the former Yugoslavia, Croatia has few severely war-injured to care for. There are no epidemics of nasty diseases spreading through the population, and even the mosquitoes carry no dangerous diseases and prefer to stay near the lakes and forests. Most importantly, nobody goes hungry. The country has abundant grain, livestock, and seafood, and Croatians temporarily down on their luck are likely to be fed by relatives, neighbors, and (such are their norms of hospitality) even by strangers.

A tradition of spa healing exists in Croatia and goes back to Roman times, when the building of *thermae* ("THER-me") began. Some of the original Roman structures are still in use; other spas are modern holiday resorts. Croatia has 14 mineral water springs, including seven thermal springs, 15 medicinal mud centers, and one medicinal oil center. Croatians believe that provided one goes to the right center, almost any human affliction can be alleviated or cured. The most commonly stated reasons for "taking the waters" are rheumatic diseases, skin problems, inflammation of the muscles, respiratory disorders, and stress. Many older Croatians go regularly to a spa.

There are about twice as many women above 65 than there are men. In 1999 there were 433,860 women over 65 years old, compared to 272,219 men above 65.

THE POSITION OF WOMEN

Women have been equal under the law in educational institutions and in the workplace since Croatia became a member of the former Yugoslavia. Fifty years later, it might be expected that women would have positions of real equality. This is not the case. A large part of the work force is female, but Croatians tend to rationalize this as a necessity in order for a family to achieve a living wage. Home tasks such as taking care of children, cooking, and cleaning are generally considered to be a woman's natural role. For many women, equality has led to a situation where they have modern rights in the workplace and traditional duties at home, leading to a greater burden for women than for men.

Young working women enjoying a drink after work.

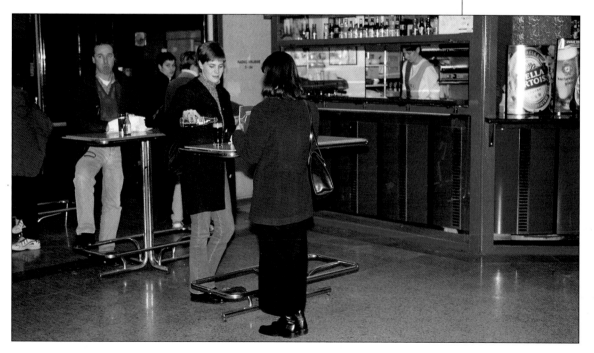

RELIGION

LIKE THE POPULATION STATISTICS on ethnicity, it is difficult to establish the number of followers of the various religions in Croatia due to the migration of people in and out of Croatia during the 1991–95 war. The official figures are either from the 1991 census, or 1995 estimates based on the 1991 figures.

According to the 1991 figures, approximately 77% of Croatians are Catholic, 11.1% are Orthodox Christian, about 1% are Muslim, 7.3% are "others" (including small Jewish and Protestant communities), and a little under 4% are atheist. Most Croats are Roman Catholics, and almost all Serbs follow the Eastern Orthodox form of Christianity.

Religion holds a special place in the hearts and minds of Croatians. Whereas politics has created centuries of division, Catholicism and Orthodox Christianity have unified the Croats and Serbs respectively since the ninth century.

Left: **An old woman selling religious trinkets.**

Opposite: **Churchgoing is very much a part of the Croatian's lifestyle.**

Above: A bishop confirm-
ing a group of young
Catholics. Today in
Croatia, almost all Croats
are Catholics.

Opposite: A grotto in a
church in Dubrovnik.

CATHOLICS

Before arriving in Croatia in the seventh century, the Croats were polytheist. Two centuries later, the Croats allied themselves to Roman Catholicism. Today, nearly all Croats are Catholics. However, for the 45 years that Croats and Serbs were united in Yugoslavia, the Croats did not parade their Catholicism. There is a historical reason for this. During World War II, the fascist *Ustaše* regime seized on religious difference to pervert the Catholic ideology and purge the population of Serbs and Jews. Extermination camps and the massacres of Serbs in villages led to reciprocal killings of Croats in Serbian areas. When Tito came to power, he suppressed religion as an active element of Yugoslav life.

In 1979, however, a large Catholic-Croatian pilgrimage to Rome was held to present a written renewal of Croatian baptismal vows. This pilgrimage celebrated centuries of Catholicism at a time when Catholics in communist Yugoslavia usually maintained a low profile in the face of official attempts to downplay religion and upgrade traditional folklore. Interestingly, the girls who carried the holy image of the Virgin Mary from Croatia to Rome were dressed in the folk costume of the island of Pag. The Pope received the pilgrims and held Mass for them in the Croatian language.

When Croatia declared independence in 1991, the Vatican was the first state to recognize the republic. Suddenly, churches were full and religious holidays were taken seriously as Croats outwardly demonstrated their identity as Catholics.

PROTESTANTS

Most Croatians in the Protestant minority belong to the Lutheran Church or the Reformed Christian Church. Protestantism first entered Croatia in the 18th century with the migration of Slovaks, Hungarians, and Germans to the area. Some were recruited to the German occupation forces in World War II. As a result, many Protestants faced persecution after the war and fled the country. Today those who remain enjoy good relations with adherents of the other religions.

ISLAM

Islam was present in Croatia even before the invasion of the Muslim Ottoman empire in the 15th and 16th centuries. Muslims were living in the eastern part of Croatia as early as the 10th century, and Islamic Turkish settlements were well established in the 12th century.

The oldest surviving mosque is in Ustikolina (now part of Bosnia and Herzegovina); it was constructed 50 years before the Turks conquered the town in 1463. The Ottoman empire did not introduce Islam but raised it to the status of a major religion among Croatians in the 15th century.

Today relations between Catholic Croatians, Muslim Croatians, and Muslim Bosnians are considered good, and Catholic and Muslim fought side by side in the wars of independence in the 1990s.

ORTHODOXY

Virtually all Serbs except atheists adhere to the Orthodox form of Christianity. Centuries-old doctrinal differences with the Catholic majority are very much alive.

Catholics worship images of the mother and child and maintain the priesthood apart from the secular world and under the Pope's authority. Orthodox Christians, on the other hand, venerate icons, allow priests to marry, and do not accept the authority or advice of the Pope.

The distinctions between Orthodox Christians and Catholics are every bit as deep as those between Catholics and Protestants, in the name of which centuries of war found political sanction in Western Europe. Like the Irish, Serbs and Croats are barely distinguishable in terms other than religion. Their conflict is thus one between Orthodox and Catholic Christians. Unfortunately there has been little attempt by religious leaders of either side to overcome conflict; at times massacres even appear to have the tacit support of religious authorities.

Below: **An Orthodox priest marks Easter by blessing a devotee.**

Opposite: **A Muslim man at prayer.**

במקום הזה עמד בית־הכנסת
המרכזי של קייק זגרב ההוקם
בשנת 1867 ונהרס על־ידי הפשי־
סטים בימי־השואה בשנת 1941

Na ovom je mjestu stajala si-
nagoga zagrebačke židovske
zajednice sagrađena 1867 i
srušena po fašističkim vla-
stima 1941 godine

JUDAISM

The first Jews are recorded to have entered Croatian cities in A.D. 723, when the Byzantine Empire expelled them. Communities of Jews settled in Split and Dubrovnik after fleeing persecution in Spain in 1491, and Portugal, in 1496. Jews living in Croatia acquired full civil rights and equality in 1873 and participated in all aspects of life in the country, excelling in the arts, sciences, and humanities, and assisting Croatia's attempts to build an education system and a modern economy.

This very good start turned bad during World War II when Croats under Nazi influence established death camps and conducted massacres of Jews and Orthodox Serbs. Between 1941 and 1945, over 80% of the Jewish population were seized and sent off to extermination camps.

More recently, Jewish Croatian numbers have been reduced by emigration, mostly to Israel and the United States, to about 2,500 people organized into nine communities. They maintain ties with Bosnian Jews to the east and south. At the birth of the 21st century, Jewish relations with other religious groups are described as good and ties with the new democratic government are strong.

MEDJUGORJE: PILGRIMAGE AND FAITH

Among the many places of local pilgrimage for Croatian Catholics, none is as popular as the Croatian village of Medjugorje, which is situated near the Croatia-Bosnia and Herzegovina border. The village contains 2,500 farmers, all Croat and firm Catholics.

On June 24 and 25, 1981, the Virgin Mary is said to have appeared at separate times to four young girls, aged 15 to 16, and two boys. It is claimed that the Madonna spoke to each, in perfect Croatian, and gave messages to be passed to the world.

Before hostilities put a temporary end to large-scale pilgrimage, over 10 million people from Croatia and elsewhere in the world visited Medjugorje. Today pilgrim numbers have again risen, although fewer pilgrims come from outside Croatia and Bosnia and Herzegovina. It is said that apparitions still occur to those who come truly seeking peace.

Left: Confession boxes for pilgrims in Medjugorje.

Opposite: This plaque marks the destruction of a synagogue.

MODNI SALON
JEANS WEST

URAR ▶

SVIJET KNJIGE
KLUPSKI CENTAR
"M. MARULIĆ"
▶▶▶▶  NAPRIJED
SPLIT
PRODAVAONICA Br. 18

 *boutique*
ŠARE
odjeća i obuća

FOTOKOPINICA - FOTOOPREMA
KARAMAN
▶▶▶▶

LANGUAGE

CROATIAN BELONGS to the South Slavic branch of the Slavic group of languages, a linguistic grouping that includes Serbian, Bosnian, and Slovene. Croatian, Serbian, and the comparative newcomer Bosnian are often referred to, as if they were one language, by the term Serbo-Croat. Precisely what constitutes a language and a dialect in the former Yugoslavia is a political rather than a linguistic question.

The speakers of any of the three languages have no trouble understanding the other two. In addition, the structure and vocabulary of the three languages are very similar.

When Croatian and Serbian are taught as foreign languages in overseas universities, it is always as a single language under the linguistic term "Serbo-Croatian." However, this term and the term "Croato-Serbian" were rejected by Croatia in the 1960s, and Croatian was considered to be a distinct language.

Left: **Young Croatians chatting in a trendy café.**

Opposite: **Croatian shop signs on a wall.**

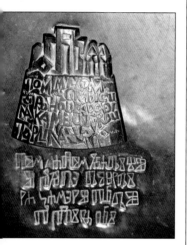

Above: An example of old Croatian script.

Opposite: An example of modern Croatian writing.

LANGUAGE OR LANGUAGES?

The similarity between Serbian and Croatian led to the Novi Sad Agreement (1954), which declared the two to be a single language with two variants. In the 1960s and 1970s, groups of Croatian and Serbian linguists independently rejected the Novi Sad Agreement, each group writing and arguing in a language they termed Croatian or Serbian, depending on which side of the ethnic divide they were on. All arguments were fully understood by the other side without any translation.

The Yugoslav authorities imposed official unity on the language(s) with a heavy hand, and in the 1980s banned and burned a number of scholarly publications maintaining that the Croatian language was a separate entity. With independence in 1991 and the subsequent war between Croatia and Serbia, the political decision that Croatian and Serbian were languages as independent as the nations that maintained them gained the upper hand. Croatian is therefore a language in its own right in the same way as Croats are people in their own right, because Croatians agree that it should be so.

HISTORICAL DEVELOPMENT

The oldest document where the Croatian language is mentioned by name dates to 1177. Croatian was not, however, the earliest indigenous language in Croatia. Before the arrival of the Croats in the seventh century, the people of Dubrovnik and neighboring coastal areas spoke Dalmatian. The use of Dalmatian disappeared in favor of Croatian in the 15th century, lingering on into the 19th century on the island of Krk.

Three regional dialects are recognized in Croatian: Kajkavian, Chakavian, and Shtokavian. Until the 15th century, the Chakavian dialect was dominant in Croatia and a large part of Bosnia. From the 17th century, the Shtokavian dialect was more widely used and over the following century became accepted as standard Croatian.

THE WRITTEN LANGUAGE

The origins of the oldest Croatian writing, known as the Glagolitic script are shrouded in time, according to some analysts. According to others, the script is clearly the invention of a Greek missionary called Cyril working in the 11th century. The argument for Cyril seems likely as he must have learned the Croatian language in order to make converts to Christianity. It appears that Cyril single-handedly constructed a script based on early Greek writing.

The earliest known example of Glagolitic script is an 11th century inscription found on Krk Island. What happened to Cyril is a mystery, but ecclesiastical works in Glagolitic continued to appear for the next two centuries.

Also in use was the Cyrillic script, originating from Greek and refined during the invention of the Russian script. Cyrillic was in use in Dubrovnik, parts of the Dalmatian coast, and Bosnia and Herzegovina. It fell out of use in the 19th century when the universal European Latin alphabet took over.

Cyrillic remains the preferred script of Serbia. Thus, the written forms of the Croatian and Serbian languages serve as national symbols dividing Croatia and Serbia.

THE SPOKEN LANGUAGE

Accepting that Croatian is a language distinct from Serbian and Bosnian (a controversy likely to continue well into the 21st century), the language is spoken by some five million people within national borders. Croatian is also spoken by at least another million Croats living in other states of the former Yugoslavia, especially in Bosnia and Herzegovina, and by an unknown proportion of up to 2.5 million ethnic Croats living overseas.

Unlike English, every letter is pronounced in Croatian, and its sound will not change from one word to another. As for which syllable of a word is stressed, the general rule is that the last syllable is never emphasized; usually, the first syllable is accented.

Children in traditional costumes gather to perform traditional Croatian folksongs.

GREETINGS

Greetings are much the same throughout countries of the former Yugoslavia. Shaking hands is universally acceptable. Touching people of the same sex is more frequent than in Western Europe or the United States; hands on shoulders and knees are tolerated. Kissing on both cheeks is more often seen between women. But kissing between men is not rare. Good friends and astute politicians may sometimes kiss on the mouth, Russian-style.

Croatian Muslims usually conform to the basic spoken pattern of *zdravo* ("ZDRAH-vo"), which means "hello," and *dovidjenja* ("DO-vee-jen-yah"), meaning "goodbye." Most are tolerant of Western European customs. Among themselves, however, Muslims will sometimes replace Croatian greetings with Arabic greetings typical in Islamic communities.

There are 1.22 million (1993 estimate) telephones in Croatia.

79

THE MEDIA

Freedom of speech is granted in Article 38 of the Constitution of the Republic of Croatia which states: "Freedom of thought and expression are guaranteed. Freedom of thought especially refers to freedom of the press and other media, freedom of speech and public appearance and founding of all the media. Censorship is forbidden by law. Journalists are entitled to free reporting and unlimited access to information. A person whose constitutional rights are violated by public information is entitled to seek redress."

NEWSPAPERS In late 1997 there were two national newspapers and nine regional dailies in Croatia. Most dailies, weeklies, biweeklies, and other periodicals are backed by private capital.

Newspapers use Croatian and the Roman (European) script. Croats do not object to publications in the Cyrillic script, as long as the contents respect Croatia and its various peoples.

Due to the strained relations with Serbia and the anti-Serbian feeling among Croats, the media generally walk a line between avoidance of comment and critical comment when Serbia is in the news. Anti-Serbian feeling does not degenerate into media hostility against Croatian Serbs, who are protected by the constitution and by a guaranteed voice in the House of Representatives.

RADIO Croatian radio stations serve national, county, or municipal communities. By January 31, 1997 Croatia had 108 licensed stations; three were national, 12 county-wide, and 93 municipal.

All the radio stations are commercial, except Croatian Radio and some nonprofit stations.

The first Croatian newspaper was the Ephemerides zagrabiense, *published in 1771. It had a circulation of 50 copies.*

TELEVISION In 1997 there were four county and seven municipal television stations; all were privately financed. This is in addition to public Croatian TV.

THE INTERNET Croatia has two Internet service providers, one academic and the other commercial. The Croatian Academic and Research Network (CARNet) provides service to educational and scientific institutions. In late 1996 CARNet was used by an estimated 60,000 people.

Internet service is also provided by HPT Internet, a unit of Croatian Telecommunications. In December 1996 it had 9,100 subscribers and 30,000 users.

A newsstand selling newspapers and periodicals.

ARTS

THE CULTURE OF CROATIA has been shaped by many things—suppression of religious beliefs, invasions by the Venetians, Austrians, Hungarians, and French, and resistance to a too-centralized government. Looking at the development of Croatian art and architecture, it is not difficult to piece together Croatia's turbulent history.

Croatian art in all its forms can be traced back over 900 years. The earliest surviving theaters, paintings, and sculpture from this time still exist in remarkable condition. Some of Croatia's earliest architecture is even older and is now attracting tourists.

Today a continuous link with the past influences the modern artist and enriches the cultural life of Croatia. Throughout the ages, folk art and crafts have survived. Now they are seen in a form and essence not so different from that initiated by the first Croats.

Left: **Musicians entertaining tourists at a ferry dock at Makarska.**

Opposite: **A street artist drawing portraits.**

MUSIC

Musical texts in neumatic notation are known to date from the 11th century, and in 1177 the Vatican records people "singing in their Croatian language."

For the next three centuries, Croatian music followed the same path of development as the rest of Europe. One notable exception is Gregorian hymns and chants, which are performed today much as they were in 14th century Croatia.

While it is known that many dramas of the 15th and 16th centuries included songs and music, usually of the folk variety, few have survived

Band players in colorful traditional costumes.

in written form. One that did was Junije Palmotić's *Atlanta* (1626), Croatia's first opera.

Secular music developed during the 18th and 19th centuries. This was in part because of the influence from Germany, and in part because of a growing movement to base music on Croatian tradition. There are many Croatian composer-musicians from this period: Elena Pucić-Sorkočević, the first female composer; Ivan Zajc, a student of Verdi who composed over 1,000 pieces of music, many of which remain popular today; and Vilko Novak, a nationalist composer who gave Croatia, *God and the Croatians* and *Hail to the Homeland*.

FILM

In 1896 the first permits for the public showing of films were issued. By 1907 permanent movie theaters existed in Zagreb, Split, Rijeka, Sisak, and Zadar. After this enthusiastic start, however, the Croatian film industry ground to a halt. This was due to the adverse economic conditions in Croatia at the beginning of the 20th century. The film industry got going again only when a need arose for film reports of military action in the 1912 Balkan Wars.

In 1917 the Croatia Film Company (which became the Yugoslavia Film Company in 1918) established in Zagreb one of the first schools for the study of film technique. However, it was not until 1933 that a Croatian director, Oktavijan Miletit, received an international cinematic award, and only after 1953 did Croatia's film industry become internationally known and acclaimed for its animated cartoons.

Outside of the cartoon genre, Croatian cinema has yet to find its place in the global scene. It remains to be seen if the upheaval of the 1990s will spur the production of movies with domestic themes.

Croatia's national string instrument is the tamburica *("TAHM-boo-ree-tzah"). The first* tamburitza *concert in the United States took place in 1900 in New York's Carnegie Hall.*

The Croatian National Theater in Zagreb.

THE PERFORMING ARTS

Croatian drama has long ties to the main European theatrical traditions. Dramas of French origin were being performed in Zagreb for the public on religious holidays in the 12th century. These early plays were based on Bible stories on the life of Christ or on legends of the saints. In spite of the religious motifs and the use of Latin by the actors, these plays contained a realistic description of everyday life.

Religion and realism continued to be linked in the 13th to the 15th centuries. One can also learn a lot about pastoral life in the past from the plays of that time, when Croatian drama was said to have come of age. Famous playwrights during the Renaissance are Mavro Vetranović (1482–1576), who wrote the first Croatian secular drama, *Diana*; Marko Marulić (1450–1524), who wrote *Judita*, the first drama to be produced in Croatian; and Marin Držić (1508–67), who was probably the first Croatian to have his work translated into other languages.

In the 17th century political commentary entered the world of drama in Ivan Gundulić's (1589–1638) epic poem *Osman*, which celebrated a 1621 victory over the Turks by the Poles. The parallel world of hated Ottoman rule and Croatian resistance was clear to every Croat who heard Gundulić's powerful words.

By the 19th century many theaters in Croatia had resident professional companies. Today watching plays in theaters has become a regular part of life for many Croatians.

PAINTING

The earliest preserved paintings, from the 11th century, are religious frescoes in the Romanesque style. In accordance with the medieval tradition, many of the artists did not sign their work. In the late 14th and early 15th centuries, Renaissance painters put their names on their masterpieces.

The mid 15th century to early 16th century is considered the best period for frescoes in Croatia, not only for their artistic merits but also because they depicted life in natural settings. The best-known wall painting from this period is the *danse macabre* (dance of death) fresco. It was completed in 1474 by Master Vincent of Kastav and decorates the church of St. Mary in Skriljine, Istria. Until the end of the 16th century, many of Croatia's artists confined themselves to the illumination of missals and other church books, but in these books, scenes from the secular and allegorical world can be found.

The interior of a theater on Hvar Island.

Zagreb became an important artistic center during the 17th century and remains so today. The 18th to 19th centuries produced attempts to blend Western European artistic achievements with the Croatian painting tradition. The most famous master of the Zagreb school was Vlaho Bukovac (1855–1922), who painted *The Croatian National Revival* on the curtain of Zagreb's Croatian National Theater.

The 20th century saw the *Monument to Peace* by Antun Augustinčić (1900–79) erected outside the United Nations building in New York City. The artistic world embraced the naive art of Croatian peasant painters like Mijo Kovačić (1935–), who produced art pieces that ordinary people found meaningful.

A mosaic found in the Euphrasian Basilica in Porec.

SCULPTURE AND ARCHITECTURE

The earliest remaining sculpture in Croatia is a three-line plaited latticework on the ninth century baptismal font of Duke Višeslav of Nin. This decoration has appeared so frequently on church doors and furniture that it has become a national symbol. Franjo Tudjman used it on posters during his first electoral campaign to signal a return to traditional Croatian culture. After the ninth century, some of the most influential sculptors were anonymous folk artists; their carvings in stone and wood appeared on almost every building and church pew. At first they depicted saints, later kings, and quickly enough peasants and contemporary life. Thus, from the beginning the arts of sculpture and architecture were intimately related. The acclaimed architecture of Croatia's churches and cathedrals is fully complemented by their exquisitely sculpted doors and portals, which combine religious scenes with the superstitions of the time in which they were crafted.

FAMOUS SCULPTORS

IVAN RENDIĆ (1849–1932) Rendić is considered the father of modern Croatian sculpture. By the time he became famous, there had been cross-fertilization of ideas and techniques. Rendić himself was a student of the great French sculptor Rodin and his works reflect his master's influence.

IVAN MEŠTROVIĆ (1883–1962) Meštrović was probably the most prominent Croatian sculptor of the 20th century. Among his world-renowned works is *Madonna with Child* (1917) in wood. An identical sculpture of work in marble is at Notre Dame University, in the United States. Meštrović moved to the United States after World War II. One of his most accomplished works there is the famous *Indians* at Grant Park in Chicago. Meštrović is often granted the greatest accolade that can be given a sculpture: his work is described as "timeless." Meštrović is buried in Otavice, Krajina (in the Šibenik-Knin region). During the 1991–95 hostilities, his grave was desecrated and some of his work damaged.

A sculpture by Meštrović out the Meštrović Art Gallery in Zagreb.

LITERATURE

The Croatian language was used for inscriptions and religious writings as early as the 11th century. Literature in Croatia, however, really got going only with the invention of the printing press in the 15th century.

Croatian writing of the 15th century falls into two categories. One continued and expanded the clerical tradition, producing legends of the many saints. The other was the humanist tradition, which produced distinguished works such as *Judita* by Marko Marulić (1450–1524). *Judita* is the first literary work written in the Croatian language by a Croatian for a Croatian audience.

In the 16th century, Croatian literature was influenced by Italy, and many poems of love, romance, and humor were written. One woman poet is mentioned in Croatian sources, Cvijeta Zuzorić (1555–99), but unfortunately none of her work has survived.

The 19th century Illyrian (National Revival) movement, which greatly influenced the work of artists, was strongly felt by Croatia's writers. This age of Romanticism gave birth to August Šenoa (1838–81), a prolific writer of historical novels, who is often called "the Croatian Sir Walter Scott."

In the 20th century, novelist and playwright Miroslav Krleža became known overseas for two famous novels, translated as *The Return of Philip Latinovicz* (1932) and the multivolume saga *Banners* (1963–65). Krleža was active in the campaign to achieve equality between Croatian and Serbian literary languages, and in 1967 opposed Tito. In contrast to Krleža, Ivo Andrić (1892–1975) used the Serbian literary dialect, lived in Belgrade, and saw himself as primarily Yugoslav and only secondarily Croat. Andrić won the Nobel Prize for Literature in 1961 for his Bosnian Trilogy: *The Bridge on the Drina*, *Bosnian Story*, and *Young Miss*.

FOLK ART

The variety of folk art in Croatia is explained by the political history of the region and the different physical environments in the country. Historically, the various Croatian regions were divided into political units and tended to come under different cultural and religious influences. The physical division into Pannonian (farmers), Alpine (herders), and Adriatic (fishers, seafarers) also meant it was possible to experience different folk costumes, songs, music, stories, and customs when moving from region to region. Today these different identities continue to exist within a greater national Croatian identity.

Physical separation has cultivated specialities sometimes limited to the confines of a small island, such as the intricate lace produced for centuries on Pag Island, the lavender products of Hvar Island, and the stone crafts on Brač Island. Similarly, each area will have its interpretation of a dance or tune, even if these have crossed original "folk" boundaries to achieve regional or national status.

The world's oldest novel on mountains is in Croatian, written by Petar Zoranić in 1536.

LACE FROM PAG ISLAND

A small 4 inch (10 cm) circle of fine Pag lace takes a skilled woman artisan up to 25 hours of work to produce. The craft probably began as a way to decorate the white linen folk costumes of the island. In the early 20th century, Pag lace became popular with Austrian nobility and gained a reputation throughout Europe. Lace-makers pass down the characteristic geometric designs through the family, adding perhaps a small personal touch that can identify an individual or a family. Pag lace is considered to be among the most delicate and durable in the world.

FOLK MUSIC

Every bit as rich as the varied folk costumes is the Croatian tradition of folk music. The traditional string instruments of the north are accompanied by guitars and accordions on the Dalmatian coast, producing an Italian sound that reflects Italy's influence on this region. Everywhere throughout Croatia can be heard the sound of the traditional *tamburica*, a three- or five-string pear-shaped mandolin. According to folklore, the Croatians brought it with them from their ancient homeland in today's Iran and Afghanistan. The *tamburica* is the national instrument of Croatia.

FOLK DANCE

Perhaps the single element nearest to a national folk activity is the *kolo* ("KO-lo"), a dance found throughout Croatia. The word *kolo* means "circle" or "wheel." The dance is marked by a large circle of men and women who move, usually in a clockwise direction, to the sound of traditional string instruments and local songs. While all dancers wear folk dress during a *kolo*, the style varies from place to place.

Above: **A** ***tamburica*, the national instrument of Croatia.**

Left: **A** *kolo* **dance, which can be described as a national dance, is often accompanied by a** *tamburica* **and other musical instruments.**

LEISURE

BEFORE THE 1991–95 WAR with Serbia and the recent conflicts among its neighbors, Croatia was a popular tourist attraction. In fact, Croatia was synonymous with the word "leisure," thanks to its natural diversity and the active promotion of cultural activities.

Croatians have at their fingertips almost the full range of leisure activities known. Some of these include listening to classical, modern, and folk music; dancing in early morning jazz clubs or discos; having a simple meal at an inn or feasting in a top-class restaurant; hunting in a virgin forest; skiing in a resort overlooking the blue Adriatic Sea; mountaineering; and water sports.

Whether they are participating or simply watching, being active or just sitting with a drink on the piazza, Croatians are never at a loss for ways to relax and enjoy life after a hard day's work.

Left: **Croatians and tourists admiring the waterfall in a national park.**

Opposite: **Yachtsmen are attracted to the Adriatic coast, especially during the long, warm summers.**

CULTURAL ACTIVITIES

For 45 years, the communist government subsidized opera, concerts, theaters, museums, and many other cultural activities to make them available to everyone. As a result of this legacy, winter evenings are warmed by the opportunity to attend national and international art events at prices that remain among the lowest in Europe.

In warm weather, Croatians can express their love for culture at summer festivals that take place in many towns. Shakespeare's *Twelfth Night* takes on a special significance when it is performed in the ancient Lovrijenas fortress in Dubrovnik—Shakespeare's setting for *Twelfth Night* is "a city in

Below: **The entrance of a museum in Zagreb is decorated by sculptures.**

Opposite: **A Sinj horse-man.**

Illyria." In Pula, the fantasy of a music recital in what is the world's third largest and arguably Europe's best-preserved Roman amphitheater is guaranteed to move any audience.

Such spectacular events were established long before tourism became significant. Today they attract an international audience and international performers.

TRADITIONAL GAMES

There are few traditional sports or games unique to Croatia. One is *balote* ("BA-lo-te"), a bowling game that developed in Dalmatia and became a favorite of the Duke of Windsor during his exile in Croatia with the American divorcee Wallis Simpson.

Another is *alka* ("AHL-kah"). Croatians call this a game, but it has been likened to a pitched battle. Held in August, *alka* involves a freely interpreted reconstruction of the defeat of the Turks in 1715 at the hands of the outnumbered Croatians of Sinj. Men on horses will try to push their lances through a row of rings hanging from a rope, all the while galloping at breakneck speed. The games provide an occasion for the *Alkali* ("AHL-kah-lee"), the renowned horsemen of Sinj, to dress up and demonstrate their horsemanship.

SPORTS

The earliest known description of a sports event in Croatia appeared in 1767 and referred to a series of fishing boat races between the cities of Split and Makarska.

Zagreb has long been the center of organized sports in Croatia. The popularity of hunting and the seeming inevitability of military conflict perhaps gave rise to the Marksmen's Society, the first sporting organization, established in 1786. This was followed after some time by a number of European-orientated sporting institutions, such as the Gymnastics Club (1874) and the Mountaineering Society (1875).

Soccer is today the country's most popular national spectator sport, with Croatia doing well against more established, better financed, and more famous clubs in the European championships. Croatia first fielded a national team in an international match in 1907, against Chechnya.

Like most European nations, Croatia has its own sports hall of fame including Olympic medal winners and recipients of other international awards. These cover a full range of sports, but Croatia excels at ball games such as basketball, soccer, water polo, tennis, and handball. Krešimir Ćosić became only the third international player ever elected to the world's Basketball Hall of Fame in Massachusetts. Dražen Petrović was another extraordinary basketball player who carried the Croatian flag in the international arena. His monument stands in Olympic Park in Lausanne, Switzerland. Recently, women have begun to make their mark internationally, with Mirjana Lucić winning the 1998 Australian Open women's doubles at the tender age of 15.

MOUNTAINEERING

It is a surprise to find such a small country competing in mountaineering. While there are Croatian peaks towering above 5,908 feet (1,800 m), mountaineers often train on Anika Kuk, a rock which stands at only 2,297 feet (700 m). Croatian Stipe Božić trained on the rock and went on to climb Mount Everest twice, the first time in 1979.

Mountaineers may train on Anika Kuk, but many will say that the most interesting challenge lies in the Velebit Mountains. This range is significant not only for its height, 5,770 feet (1,758 m), but for its overall size. Velebit is 90 miles (145 km) long, 6 to 19 miles (10 to 30 km) wide and covers an area of 878 square miles (2,274 square km). It is steep, mostly bare of vegetation, and rich in caves, making it an ideal location for a real mountaineering trial.

NAUTICAL TOURISM

Sailing and diving are very popular with both Croatians and foreigners. Croatia has 40 marinas, fully equipped with services, shops, and restaurants, and serving over 12,300 officially berthed vessels. Several marinas run sailing schools that are popular with Croatians, many of whom own some sort of seagoing vessel.

A growing number of Croatians are joining foreign tourists who are intrigued as much by what is under the surface as by what is above it. Numerous diving schools exist, and Croatia provides the clearest, safest, and nearest sea for Europeans interested in learning the sport or simply experiencing the underwater world of colorful fish and corals.

HUNTING

Croatia contains virgin forest that is the envy of other European countries. Some 50% of Croatia is set aside for 768 hunting preserves. Twenty-five thousand licenses are allocated for the hunting of big game (deer, wild boar, and bear) and 320,000 for small game (pheasant, partridge, and hare).

While Croatian men are hunting for meat, particularly welcome in a time of economic trouble, Croatian women may be gathering truffles and other natural foods. Croatians enjoy a long tradition of hunting for both food and sport. It is possible to retain this aspect of national culture because of the favorable ratio of population to resources.

Unfortunately, there are already signs that Croatia's current economic difficulties are putting pressure on the timber and furniture export industries to expand, leading to rapid denudation of forests. And even the most pro-gressive system of forest reserves can do little against the destructive effects of acid rain creeping down from Croatia's industrialized northern neighbors.

The Croatian farmer or worker may feel that the woods are full of game, but there is no guarantee that this traditional cultural pastime and family budget-stretcher will continue forever.

Left: **Deer are one type of game hunted by Croatians.**

Opposite: **Sailing boats anchored at a dock.**

HEALTH SPAS

Croatians advancing in years, sportsmen relaxing their muscles, and anybody seeking a cure for or relief from a variety of health problems can be found in Croatia's many thermal springs. Many young Croatians also follow the tradition of their parents and ancestors and regularly drink or relax in the waters. All will testify that the Croatians' good standard of health owes much to the spa habit.

Medical opinion seems to confirm the beneficial effects of spa water generally and of the healing quality of Ivanic Grad's mud baths in particular. This famous mud is said to heal psoriasis, a chronic, inflammatory skin disease.

A woman having a mud facial treatment.

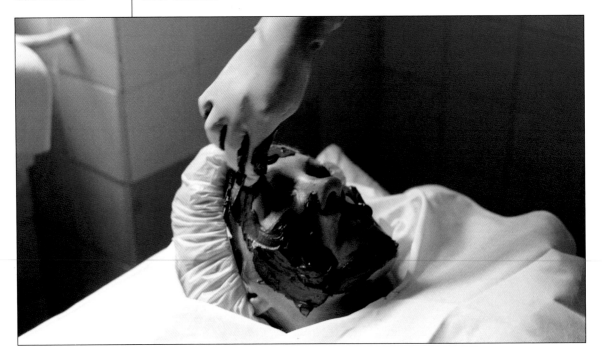

PILGRIMAGE

After 45 years of keeping a low religious profile, Croatians are now making pilgrimages to Trsat (in Rijeka), Sinj, and many other famous national sanctuaries. Although religious in essence, the trips also provide a focus for a family day out and serve a leisure function because pilgrimages are usually social and recuperative.

After a vicious war with Serbian neighbors, and a continuing bad economic situation that is largely beyond Croatia's control, pilgrimages provide a certain catharsis for people. It is better to do something to improve a situation than to do nothing at all, and Croatians are not known to sit and brood.

A church in Medjugorje, a popular destination for pilgrims.

NIGHTLIFE

For those Croatians who can afford it, nightclubs, casinos and discos are places to go at night. More Croatian in mood, and more in line with the average Croat's budget, are the folk and jazz clubs. All such clubs may remain open until 4 a.m.

An alternative activity is the *kino* ("KEE-no"), the low-priced and very popular cinema, where Croatians watch mostly foreign films in the original soundtrack. A *kino* may show several different movies in one evening, starting with family entertainment and moving on to more adult themes later in the evening and past midnight.

On delightful summer nights, many Croatians prefer to remain outdoors, taking a stroll on the town piazza and drinking Croatian wine at one of the many open-air restaurants.

SHOPPING

Two of the mysteries of modern Croatia are how a struggling economy manages to stock such a wide variety of shops with mostly imported clothing and how a financially strapped people appear as if they have just purchased these smart outfits to wear to the office or for an evening of leisure.

The economic difficulties that followed the war and Croatia's independence have not stopped Croatians from shopping; quite the opposite. Intent on stretching their kuna as far as possible, Croatians spend more time in the shops than they ever did, trying on more clothes before finally settling on a purchase. If shopping is now more expensive, Croatians cut down on their trips to the fashion houses of Italy and are even more determined to get value for their money, and to enjoy doing so.

Shops at a popular mall in Zagreb.

FESTIVALS

SINCE INDEPENDENCE, traditional Croatian culture has been celebrated and promoted, especially traditional songs, dances, and festivals. Festivals and celebrations in Croatia tend to fall into two types: the national, observed throughout the country, and the local, organized by and sometimes peculiar to a town, an island, or an area.

Each town has its own carnival. Perhaps the most elaborate and longest are those held in Samobor, a town known for its folk traditions and crafts, and Rijeka, where businesses close and the entire town gives itself up to seven days of celebrations at the beginning of Lent every year. Carnivals to mark the beginning of Lent are colorful and exciting, with music, dancing, and dressing up in traditional folk costumes being the order of the day. Most festivals take place during the summer months of July and August. Some annual events are fixed on the calendar, while others are held every year at approximately the same time.

Left: Traditional costumes are as much a part of festivals as singing and dancing.

Opposite: **Masks, paint, horns, and hats—all these add up to the spirit of fun during a festival.**

RELIGIOUS FESTIVALS

Many traditions that have been revived since Croatia's independence are religious in nature, for example, Lent and Easter. Every year more Croatians commemorate Lent, and the celebrations are growing bigger with elaborate and spectacular processions that attract visitors from within and outside Croatia.

Croatians appear to be unanimous in the choice of their favorite and most significant festival: Christmas. It is observed by the great majority of Croatians, who will gather with the extended family to celebrate with joy and feasting, both privately at home in the company of relatives, and

Below: **Although Christmas is celebrated in different ways around the world, Santa Claus is always recognizable.**

Opposite: **The annual Poklad festival held on Lastovo Island.**

publicly in packed church services and with neighborhood carolers. As in other ceremonies and festivals, the Croatian identity is reinforced during this time.

Holy Week, which is the week before Easter, is another occasion when neighbors and townspeople gather together for festivities. On the islands of Brač, Hvar, and Korčula, celebrations come in the form of processions. In central Croatia, people light bonfires to mark Holy Week.

TRADITIONAL FESTIVALS

The origins of some popular traditional festivals are lost over time, as with the crossbow competition held on Rab Island on July 27, where men in colorful Renaissance clothing compete to shoot arrows at targets. Remembrance Day, the Sunday nearest May 15, is certainly not forgotten in the town of Sinj. On this day the victims of Croatia's wars are remembered, and at the same time, an old Croatian victory over the army of the Ottoman empire is celebrated in a series of spirited games and festivities. Events conclude in a competition between Sinj horsemen to spear hanging rings with the tip of a lance while riding at full gallop.

NONRELIGIOUS FESTIVALS

Croatia has many nonreligious festivals, and most occur in the summer. These festivals not only attract tourists but Croatians to the cities where the festivals are held to enjoy the festivities and the warm summer nights.

SUMMER FESTIVALS The most prestigious festival in Croatia is the Dubrovnik Summer Festival, which started in 1950. Taking place from mid-July to mid-August, this festival showcases theater, concerts, and dance in several open-air locations around the city. Besides Dubrovnik, Zagreb, Split, and Osor (a town on Cres Island) also have their own summer festivals.

The Dubrovnik Summer Festival attracts many people annually.

CHILDREN'S FESTIVAL In the city of Šibenik there is a festival just for children. The International Children's Festival starts in the last week of June or in the first week of July. There are workshops in crafts, music, dance, children's film, and theater.

ARTS FESTIVALS In Zagreb, there is a Festival of Animated Films, which takes place in even-numbered years. A Festival of Art is held in Rovinj, where painters get the opportunity to display their work.

CROATIAN NATIONAL HOLIDAYS

January 1	New Year's Day
January 6	Epiphany
March/April	Easter Monday
May 1	May Day
Sunday nearest May 15	Remembrance Day
May 30	Independence Day
June 22	Anti-Fascist Day
August 5	Homeland Thanksgiving Day
August 15	Assumption
November 1	All Saints' Day
December 25 & 26	Christmas

SPECIAL HOLIDAYS FOR MINORITIES

Serbs : Orthodox Christmas (January 7) and Orthodox Easter
Muslims : Ramadan Bajram and Kurban Bajram
Jews : Rosh Hashana (Jewish New Year) and Yom Kippur

(All holidays are moveable on the Gregorian calendar except for Orthodox Christmas)

The Moreska Sword Dance has been performed on Korčula Island since the 15th century to commemorate Korčula Town Day (July 29). The dance tells of the fight between two kings to win a princess.

111

FOOD

CROATIAN FOOD REFLECTS the country's varied history, which has clearly been influenced by its neighbors' cuisine. At the same time, Croatian cuisine manages to maintain an essence of Croatia that allows each region to express its special flavor.

The Dalmatian coast enjoys a Mediterranean climate and a Mediterranean diet that consists mainly of seafood, boiled or grilled on open fires and seasoned with olive oil and a variety of herbs. The food is often served with rice and washed down with strong red wine. On the other hand, the continental north, which experiences cold winters, serves up hearty meat dishes, accompanied by potatoes and a light wine.

There is no lack of places to eat in Croatia. Depending on their budget, Croatians can choose to patronize fast food joints that serve local snacks or Western food, or restaurants that dish out fancier fare.

Left: **A rainbow selection of olive oil flavored with various fruits, vegetables, and spices.**

Opposite: **Smoking freshly caught fish.**

Traditional cooked meats and sausages in a shop window.

FOREIGN INFLUENCE

Italy, just a few miles across the Adriatic Sea from Dalmatia, has strongly influenced the food in the coastal region. Pizza, spaghetti, and risotto are as easily found here as in Italy. A typical meal would begin with thin slivers of smoked ham as an appetizer, followed by *prstaci* ("prer-STAH-tsee"), a pasta topped with seafood, or *brodet* ("BRO-det"), a mixed fish stew with rice.

The tastes of Hungary, Austria, and Turkey are readily discernible in the north and east. Croatians in the Zagreb region expect plenty of meat on their plates. Pork, lamb, turkey, and duck are roasted, very often on a spit in the traditional fashion. Veal steaks are stuffed with ham and cheese and fried in breadcrumbs.

A typical inland meal is not light on calories. Even in modest households, the main meal of the day, eaten either at noon or in the evening, may begin with baked cheese dumplings called *štrukli* ("SHTROOklee") or a simple potato soup. This may be followed by *gulaš* ("GOO-lahsh"), or goulash, as much a staple in this part of Croatia as it is in Hungary, and finished off with *palačinka* ("PAH-lah-cheen-kah"), pancakes filled with jam and topped with chocolate.

The eastern Slavonia region is known for its liberal use of paprika and garlic. Here the meat diet is varied with river fish, mostly carp and pike, traditionally steamed in paprika sauce and served with noodles. *Kulen* ("KOO-len"), a paprika-flavored sausage, is eaten as a snack or served with cottage cheese, peppers, pickled vegetables, and chunks of bread as an evening meal. Cakes stuffed with walnuts, poppy seeds, and plum jam often mark the end of a meal.

A family at the dinner table. Besides eating utensils, Croatians use their hands to pick up food with a piece of bread.

Croatians have many ways to spice up their food.

REGIONAL SPECIALITIES

Croatia is one of the few countries in Europe that continues to enjoy fresh game from under-exploited forests, fresh fish from large territorial salt waters, mountain lakes, and rivers, and truffles and other less exotic mushrooms fresh from the wooded hills of Istria. Such abundance has left its mark on eating habits.

At the beginning of the 21st century, as Croatia strives for economic advance, many of the finest delicacies are exported and beyond everyday consumption for the average Croatian. However, when family, religious, or festive occasions bring Croatians together, conspicuous feasting on the finest the region has to offer remains the order of the day.

Regional specialities still very much part of Croatian diets include: *visovačka begavica* ("VEE-so-vahtch-kah BE-gah-vee-tsah"), a savory lamb cooked in ewe's milk in the Šibenik area; *mlinci* ("MLEEN-tsee"), flat sour dumplings served with turkey around Zagreb and in northwestern

Croatia; *zagorska zlevka* ("ZAH-gor-skah ZEH-lev-kah"), cornflour cake from the Zagorje area, north of Zagreb; pungent hard cheese served with olives on Pag Island; and *tartufi* ("TAHR-too-fee"), wild truffles on a pasta base, in the Istria area.

Snack food is cheap and common in all towns throughout the country. It is often of Turkish origin. Some examples are *ćevapčići*, ("CHE-vahp-chee-chee"), or spicy beef or pork meatballs, *ražnjići* ("RAHZH-nyee-chee"), or kebab, and *burek* ("BOO-rek"), or pastry stuffed with either meat or cheese.

THE KITCHEN

The kitchen is the heart of a Croatian home and the domain of the wife and mother. Today's modern kitchen differs little from that of other countries. In the mountains or the more remote agricultural areas and islands, an electric stove may still be an unnecessary luxury, since firewood provides the main fuel for cooking and heating.

BREAKFAST

Croatians generally eat two heavy meals a day. They usually skip breakfast, but if they do not, it is likely to be a cold slice of rich *burek* and a strongly brewed espresso coffee served in a tiny cup.

DESSERT

It is difficult to find a Croatian who does not have a sweet tooth, and an abundance of cakes satisfies this craving. Many people feel that dinner is incomplete without the ubiquitous *orahnjača* ("o-RAH-nyah-chah"), yeast rolls made with plenty of sugar and ground walnuts.

Below: **Shops like these, selling chocolates, are popular with Croatians.**

Opposite: **A winemaker on the island of Korčula.**

DRINKS

Alcoholic drinks are a normal accompaniment to the main meal of the day, whether it is eaten at home or in a restaurant, and Croatia offers a wide variety of brandies, wines, and beer. Nonalcoholic drinks include strong coffee and a range of herbal teas.

Croatia is known for *šljivovica* ("shel-YEE-vo-vee-tsah"), a famous plum brandy taken before a meal; *vinjak* ("VEEN-yahk"), cognac drunk as a pick-me-up, often with strong coffee; and *maraschino* ("mah-rah-SKEE-no"), a cherry liqueur from Zadar and *prosecco* ("pro-SETS-tso"), a sweet dessert wine. The country's oldest vineyards are found in Dalmatia. Eastern Slavonia produces excellent white wines, including the famous label Kutjevačka Graševina.

Foreigners often joke that Croatians can turn wine into water. This refers to the national habit of diluting wine in the glass with water, a peculiarity for which no logical explanation exists. It is simply a Croatian habit.

Pivo ("PEE-vo"), or beer, is every bit as popular as wine. Fewer varieties exist, but Karlovačko beer from Karlovac is generally regarded as the best. Whatever the drink, it is normal behavior to raise glasses to those around and say *živjeli* ("ZHIV-ye-lee"), or "cheers!"

EATING OUT

Croatians love to eat with company and much regret that recent economic difficulties require a high degree of self-restraint when it comes to eating out. On the bright side, economic hardship at home and a sharp drop in tourism means prices remain comparatively low, while quality stays high. Thus, Croatians are frequently tempted to break self-imposed spending limits and find occasions to eat out.

By far the most popular place to gather is the *gostionica* ("gos-TEEO-nee-tsah") or *konoba* ("KO-no-bah"). Both terms mean "restaurant-pub." *Restauracija* ("RES-tah-oo-rah-tsee-yah"), or "restaurants proper," tend to

Pizza is a good, cheap meal in Croatia.

be slightly more expensive and have lost out in the competition to provide quality food and drink in the quantities that Croatians demand in exchange for their hard-earned kuna. In the *restauracija* there is no minimum order; families or individuals may sit for hours with a beer and snack or order a full meal of several courses accompanied by the finest wines. The pocket and self-discipline decide.

Self-service cafeterias have caught on in towns, particularly Zagreb, and they offer good, cheap food but a less social atmosphere. They are popular in Croatia as convenient and quick places for lunch.

BRODET

Fish stew Istriana-style. Serves 2 to 4.

Ingredients
$^1/_4$ cup olive oil
1 white fish (snapper or sea bass)
$2^1/_4$ lbs (1 kg) mixed shellfish
$^1/_3$ lbs (150 g) squid, cut into small rounds
onion, sliced
4 cloves garlic
2 to 3 tomatoes, quartered
parsley, chopped, chopped
2 bay leaves
salt and pepper
2 cups water
$^1/_2$ cup white wine

Heat olive oil in a large pot and saute the fish until brown. Add shellfish and squid, onion, garlic, tomatoes, parsley, bay leaves, salt and pepper. Add water. Bring to a boil. Add wine and simmer for 30 minutes, stirring occasionally. Serve with pasta, rice, or bread.

CROATIA

A   **B**   **C**   **D**

0   20   40   60   80 Miles
0   20   40   60   80   100 Kilometers

1

HUNGARY

Drava

Danube

SLOVENIA

●Varaždin

●Krapina

Medvednica Mountains

CROATIA - SLAVONIA   ●Bjelovar

●ZAGREB   *Pannonian Plain*   ●Virovitica

●Samobor

Sava

Papuk Mountains

Drava

SERB

2

Gulf of Venice

ISTRIA

Opatija●   ●Rijeka

Porec●

Istrian Peninsula

Rovinj●

Kupa   ●Karlovac   ●Sisak

●Glina

Psunj Mountains

Sava

●Osijek

●Vukovar

Danu

Krk

●Pula

Cres

Velika Kapela Mountains

Plitvice Lakes

Plieševića Mountains

3

Rab

Lošinj

Pag

Velebit Mountains

DALMATIA

Mount Dinara (6,006 ft/1,830 m)

BOSNIA AND HERZEGOVINA

N

●Zadar

Ugljan

Dugi Otok

Pašman

Krka●   ▲

●Knin

Dinaric Alps

Kornat

Cetina

●Šibenik

●Sinj

4

ITALY

Trogir●   ●Split

Brač

●Makarska

Neretva

Hvar

●Medjugorje

Ploče●

Korčula

Pelješac

MONTENE

A d r i a t i c

●Ston

● Capital city
● Major town
▲ Mountain peak

Lastovo   *Mljet*   Dubrovnik●

Feet	Meters
3,300	1,000
1,650	500
660	200
0	0

S e a

Gulf of Kotor

5

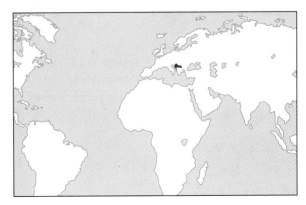

QUICK NOTES

OFFICIAL NAME
Republic of Croatia (*Republika Hrvatska*)

TOTAL AREA
21,824 square miles (56,538 square km)

POPULATION
4.7 million (July 1999 estimate)

POPULATION GROWTH RATE
0.1% (1999 estimate)

CAPITAL
Zagreb

MAJOR CITIES
Dubrovnik, Rijeka, Šibenik, Spilt, Zadar

MAJOR ISLANDS
Brač, Cres, Hvar, Korčula, Krk, Pelješac

MAJOR RIVERS
Drava, Neretva, Sava

CLIMATE
Mediterranean and continental

MOUNTAIN RANGES
Dinaric Alps, Medvednica Mountains, Papuk Mountains, Plješevica Mountains, Psunj Mountains, Velebit Mountains, Velika Kapela Mountains

HIGHEST POINT
Mount Dinara (6,006 feet/1,830 m)

MAIN RELIGIONS
Roman Catholicism, Christian Orthodoxy

OFFICIAL LANGUAGE
Croatian

CURRENCY
The Croatian kuna (KN)
US$1 = 6.42 KN (1999)

MAIN EXPORTS
Oil, food and beverages, textiles, electrical appliances

MAIN IMPORTS
Machinery and transport equipment, miscellaneous manufactured articles, chemicals

IMPORTANT POLITICAL LEADERS
Dr. Franjo Tudjman—First president
Stipe Mesić—Current president
Ivica Račan—Prime minister

NATIONAL FLAG
Red, white, and blue horizontal bands with a Croatian coat of arms in the center (25 red and white checks on a shield and crown made up of former emblems of Croatia, Dubrovnik, Dalmatia, Istria, and Slavonia

IMPORTANT HOLIDAYS
Independence Day—May 30
Day of Antifascist Struggle—June 22
Homeland Thanksgiving Day—August 5
All Saints' Day—November 1

GLOSSARY

alka ("AHL-kah")
A Croatian game played in Sinj, which celebrates the 1715 defeat of the Turks

breks ("BREKS")
Truffle-hunting dogs.

brodet ("BRO-det")
Istriana-style fish stew.

burek ("BOO-rek")
A rich pastry stuffed with meat or cheese.

dovidjenja ("DO-vee-jen-yah")
A Croatian word for "goodbye."

Glagolitic script
An ancient Croatian writing probably invented by a Greek missionary, Cyril.

gostionica ("gos-TEEO-nee-tsah")
A family-run restaurant.

kino ("KEE-no")
A low-priced and very popular cinema where Croatians watch mostly foreign films.

kolo ("KO-lo")
A Slavic dance where people dance in a circle.

kotari ("ko-TAH-ree")
Districts.

kulen ("KOO-len")
A Paprika sausage.

kuna ("KOO-nah")
The Croatian currency.

orahnjača ("o-RAH-nyah-chah")
Yeast rolls made with sugar and ground walnuts.

palačinka ("PAH-lah-cheen-kah")
Pancakes filled with jam and topped with chocolate.

pivo ("PEE-vo")
Beer.

ražnjići ("rahzh-NYEE-chee")
Kebab.

Sabor ("SAH-bor")
The Croatian Parliament.

šljivovica ("shel-YEE-vo-vee-tsah")
A famous plum brandy drunk before a meal.

tamburica ("TAHM-boo-ree-tsah")
A three- or five-string mandolin.

Ustaše ("OOS-tah-she")
The World War II fascist regime in Croatia.

zdravo ("ZDRAH-vo")
A Croatian word for "hello."

živjeli ("ZHIV-ye-lee")
A Croatian word for "cheers," or a toast.

županijas ("zhoo-PAH-nee-yahs")
Regional counties.

BIBLIOGRAPHY

Bartulin, Boris, et al. *Croatia*. Madrid: Croatian Ministry of Foreign Affairs, 1996.

Croatia Weekly. Zagreb: Croatian Institute for Culture and Information.

Cuvalo, Ante (ed). *Croatia and the Croatians*. Zagreb: North Tribune Publishing, 1991.

Kapetanic, Sanja. *Croatia Your Partner*. Zagreb: Croatian Chamber of Commerce, 1998.

Oliver, Jeanne. *Croatia (Lonely Planet Series)*. Hawthorn, Australia: Lonely Planet Publications Pte Ltd, 1999.

Silber, Laura & Little, Allan. *The Death of Yugoslavia*. London: BBC Books, 1995.

INDEX

INDEX

INDEX

PICTURE CREDITS